EVERY

FALLING

STAR

SUNGJU LEE

& SUSAN McCLELLAND

AMULET BOOKS

NEW YORK

EVERY

FALLING

STAR

THE TRUE STORY OF HOW I SURVIVED
AND ESCAPED NORTH KOREA

Library of Congress Cataloging-in-Publication Data

Names: Lee, Sungju. | McClelland, Susan.
Title: Every falling star : how I survived and escaped North Korea / by
Sungju Lee and Susan Elizabeth McClelland.
Description: New York : Amulet Books, 2016.
Identifiers: LCCN 2016002463 (print) | LCCN 2016014432 (ebook) | ISBN
9781419721328 (hardback) | ISBN 9781613123409 ()
Subjects: LCSH: Lee, Sungju—Childhood and youth—Juvenile literature. | Lee,
Sungju—Family—Juvenile literature. | Boys—Korea
(North)—Biography—Juvenile literature. | Homeless boys—Korea
(North)—Biography—Juvenile literature. | Street children—Korea
(North)—Biography—Juvenile literature. | Survival—Korea
(North)—Juvenile literature. | Korea
(North)—History—1994-2011—Biography—Juvenile literature. | Korea
(North)—Social conditions—Juvenile literature. | BISAC: JUVENILE
NONFICTION / Biography & Autobiography / Cultural Heritage. | JUVENILE
NONFICTION / Biography & Autobiography / Political. | JUVENILE NONFICTION
/ People & Places / Asia. | JUVENILE NONFICTION / Social Issues /
Homelessness & Poverty.
Classification: LCC DS935.7773.L44 A3 2016 (print) | LCC DS935.7773.L44
(ebook) | DDC 951.9305/1092—dc23
LC record available at http://lccn.loc.gov/2016002463

Text copyright © 2016 Sungju Lee
Book design by Julia Marvel

Printed and bound in U.S.A.
10 9 8 7 6 5 4 3 2 1

Amulet Books are available at special discounts when purchased in quantity for
premiums and promotions as well as fundraising or educational use.
Special editions can also be created to specification. For details, contact
specialsales@abramsbooks.com or the address below.

ABRAMS The Art of Books
115 West 18th Street, New York, NY 10011
abramsbooks.com

I DEDICATE THIS BOOK TO THOSE I LEFT BEHIND
IN NORTH KOREA.

—Sungju Lee

Some family names have been changed to protect relatives still living in North Korea. The names of my brothers, though, are real, in the hope that they are still alive and will read this book.

Until we meet again.

—Sungju Lee

A BRIEF HISTORY OF 20TH-CENTURY KOREA

For thousands of years, successive dynasties and monarchs ruled the Korean Peninsula. The last and most influential dynasty was the Joseon. In 1876, the Japanese coerced Korea to sign a treaty that eventually ended the Joseon Dynasty. Under the Japanese, the Korean people were largely oppressed. Former landowners were pushed off their properties, and others were forced to work as slave laborers for Japanese overlords. Many of the houses, monuments, and buildings built during the Joseon Dynasty, and most of its traditions, were destroyed. Japan, which occupied the Korean Peninsula from 1910 to 1945, sought to integrate the region into its own empire.

With the defeat of Japan at the end of World War II, Japan's territories were taken away. The Korean Peninsula was divided into two separate, yet temporary, governments and economic zones: the North, which was overseen by the Soviet Union, and the South, which was overseen by the United States. The plan was to unite the two regions into one with a general democratic election. The Soviet Union placed guerrilla army leader Kim Il-sung, who had returned from exile in China in 1945, as head of the North's temporary government. He managed to persuade the Soviets not to take part in any election. He clung to socialism and rejected American-style democracy. He felt the entire region should be communist.

In 1948, the South was granted independence from the United States, becoming the Republic of Korea. Shortly thereafter, the North became the Democratic People's Republic of Korea, or North Korea. North Koreans refer to their country as Joseon, after the last dynasty. Like its namesake today, the Joseon Dynasty was dubbed the "Hermit Kingdom" because it sealed itself off from the world in an attempt to ward off invasion.

The political and economic systems of the two nations couldn't be more different. The South has a democratic government and a capitalist, free-market economy. North Korea, on the other hand, is a communist state, with one political party and no elections. Most things, including property, are publicly owned. Until the breakdown of the state's food-ration program in the early 1990s, all food, clothes, and necessities—including housing—were allocated by the state, based on an individual's need and standing within the Communist Party.

Kim Il-sung believed that it was only a matter of time before the ideology of the North swept the South. He believed that the two regions would unite under communism. He was convinced that South Korea was funded by—indeed, was a "puppet nation" of—the United States. The Korean War, from June 1950 to July 1953, involved a United States–backed South Korea vying to unify the entire peninsula under its government versus the Soviet-backed North Korea aiming to do the same.

Aside from the war, which resulted in few geographical changes but a dramatic increase in tensions between the South and the North, the early years of Kim Il-sung were not that bad for North Korean people. There was a revival in the arts; the creation of monuments, museums, buildings, hotels, and theme parks; work, including an increase in farming and industry; and plenty of food through the centralized ration system.

Kim Il-sung gained a cult following during his years as leader of North Korea, largely because of the dissemination of books, films, radio, and television shows that made the people distrust Westerners, China, and Japan and revere, almost like a god, their leader and his life and government. All television and news outlets were monitored by the government; the result was that the state and Kim Il-sung were described only in positive terms. Deniers and critics of the regime were sent to political and/or labor camps, often with their entire families.

In the 1990s, North Korea suffered several blows. First there was the breakdown of the communist state of the Soviet Union in 1991. The many countries under its rule were allowed to form their own governments. (The Soviet Union itself become the pseudo-democratic country of Russia.) As a result, North Korea lost its main trading partner and its primary source of aid. Then a series of weather anomalies resulted in devastating floods, which caused a shortage of domestically grown products. If this wasn't enough to drive the nation into famine, the breakdown in the central ration system certainly did. On July 8, 1994, Kim Il-sung died. His son, Kim Jong-il, became his successor. Kim Jong-il was poorly equipped to deal with these strains.

The country plummeted into a famine that some estimate killed more than a million of its approximately twenty-four million people. In a desperate attempt to save their lives, North Koreans began to leave the country. It's nearly impossible to escape North Korea by heading directly to South Korea because the border between the two countries is heavily mined with explosives. Therefore, the main escape route is through China to Mongolia, Laos, or Thailand. China, however, does not recognize North Koreans as refugees but, rather, as illegal work migrants. Any North Koreans found in China are returned, where they face prison for trying to escape.

North Korea is indeed a Hermit Kingdom: a true-to-life dystopian nation.

It's against this backdrop that my story takes place.

y toy soldier peers over a mound of dirt not far from where my father, *abeoji*, my mother, *eomeoni*, and I have just finished our picnic, near the Daedong River in Pyongyang.

My father and I are setting up the toy soldiers to reenact one of the decisive battles in which our eternal leader, Kim Il-sung, ousted the Japanese army from our country, Joseon—or, as most in the West know it, North Korea. My father is in charge of the Japanese troops. My own troops are separated, with part of my army standing behind my general. The rest are hidden in a bush near the river. My father's army is positioned in the middle.

I am carrying a wooden pistol that my father carved and painted for me. My mother is playacting as my army nurse. The blanket on which we had our picnic is now the hospital.

My father has drawn a thick Hitler-like mustache on his general using my *eomeoni*'s eyebrow pencil. She's not happy because he broke the pencil's tip. In fact, every time my father and I play war games, he uses—and ruins—her makeup to decorate his toy soldiers.

"Okay, your general will be our eternal leader, Kim Il-sung," my mother snaps. She is very testy today. She really wants to defeat my father. "Since we don't have telephones or walkie-talkies, our troops need a way to communicate with each other. So take these." She slips some smooth stones into my hand. I know what she is about to say next. She is going to use my father's own military tactics, which he taught me during other war games, against him.

"Designate one of your soldiers to be in charge of relaying your general's orders to your troops who are trapped on the other side of the Japanese. This soldier must sneak through the forest and, at the big rock," my mother says, pointing, "lay stones so that your other troops know what the eternal leader wants them to do. The stones are codes. One stone means stand down, it's too dangerous to attack; two stones mean get ready; three stones mean attack the Japanese when the moon hits the sky at the highest point in the night."

I bow to my mother and pick up one of my sergeants. I make him my guerrilla messenger. He will steal through the pine and oak trees, leaving my coded stone orders by the big rock.

I can feel it in the air. *Victory*. After all, Joseon always wins. We are the best country on earth!

I'm six years old.

Little do I know this military tactic will one day come to save my life.

CHAPTER

1

dream. And in my dream, I'm a general in the army of the Democratic People's Republic of Korea. I'm leading my unit in the April 25 parade celebrating the foundation of the Korean People's Army. Our leader, Kim Il-sung, formed the army in 1932. Well, back then, the army was really nothing more than bands of guerrillas. Today, it's one of the largest armies in the world, with nearly nine million members. Our country's population is only about twenty-five million, so that's a lot of our people in the military.

Okay . . . back to my dream. The main road in the nation's capital, Pyongyang, in front of Kim Il-sung Square, is lined with people cheering and waving white magnolias and long cherry blossom stems. The entire city has come out for the parade. They always do.

Wearing the uniform of the North Korean army, my chest held high and showcasing line after line of my badges, I march, my sword by my side. My gun, the semiautomatic Baekdu, named after the birthplace of my eternal leader's son, Kim Jong-il, is held stiffly across my body. My eyes are focused, like lasers, in front of me. My knees swing high as the band behind me performs the song "Parade of Victory."

While I don't look at them directly, the women in the crowd wear traditional North Korean dresses in colors reserved for such special occasions: floor-length puffy dresses with ribbons in soft pinks, baby blues, and rich creams. I also know that yellow, orange, and white balloons dance across the cloudless azure sky.

I turn my face only when we pass the stage at Kim Il-sung Square, where our supreme leader, Kim Il-sung, stands. I salute. I know he is looking on with pride. My entire unit is polished, walking in precision, servants to him, our eternal father, protecting our nation from South Korean invasion, ruthless Japanese expansion, and the American culture of excess that threatens our way of life.

Joseon is the best nation in the world, and in my dream I am so proud of being able to give back and make North Korea even safer.

That dream was long ago, when I lived in a large apartment not far from Kim Il-sung Square. My father was in the army. It was my destiny to follow in his footsteps. I was being raised to be a military officer in the Korean People's Army just like him. He held a high position, and I would, too.

OUR APARTMENT HAD A REFRIGERATOR THAT WAS ALWAYS
stocked with meats and fresh vegetables. We had a color television and a baby grand piano on which my mother played the folk
songs "*Arirang*" and "*So-nian-jang-soo.*"

Our home had three bedrooms, but while I had my own room,
every second or third night I would creep into my parents' room
and snuggle in between my mother and father. I liked smelling
my mother's lavender and rose perfume, faint on her clothes and
pillow, and feeling my father's musk-scented breath on my cheek.
Lying between them made me feel safe from the monsters that I
learned at school were always wanting to invade my country and
enslave me: the Americans, the Japanese, and the South Korean
army, which, of course, is controlled by the United States.

In a small house right beside our apartment building lived
my dog, Bo-Cho, which means "guard." Bo-Cho was a Pungsan,
bred in the mountains of Ryanggang Province. Pungsans are rare,
and only special boys got them as pets, or so my mother told me.
On summer nights, when the crickets chirped and I fanned my
face with my hands to keep cool, I would sneak down and curl up
beside Bo-Cho, nestling in close to his soft white fur. With our
heads poking out the front door of his doghouse, his facing down
and resting on his paws, mine looking up at the stars, I'd talk to
him about *Boy General*, the best television cartoon in Joseon. "The
show is set during the Goguryeo Dynasty, which, so you know,

ran from about 900 to 1400," I would explain. "The boy general's father passed away in the battlefield. When the father was killed, his sword went to his son, who became a great boy general and defeated many invaders. The story means that boys can be strong and protect their country, too."

I'd awake in the mornings with the soft dew dampening my face and clothes, and I'd return to my bedroom before my mother and father knew I was even gone.

My father had a big important job. But exactly what he did in the military I never knew then, and I don't want to say now, because we may still have relatives in Joseon who could face imprisonment if the government found out I was sharing my story. When my father wore his uniform, I'd stare at all his badges, particularly the stripes and stars indicating his rank, and his awards for bravery. In the mornings, I would imitate him, sipping black tea and reading the *Rodong Sinmun*, the newspaper of the Central Committee of the Workers' Party of Korea, followed by the *Joseon Inmingun*, the newspaper of the Korean People's Army.

When the humid summer air turned fresh again, I knew school was just around the corner. On those mornings, I'd don my school uniform and leave the apartment with my father, holding his hand as I skipped down the stairs. We'd say goodbye outside; then he went his way and I went mine. But I would often stop and watch him as he walked down the road. His gait was crisp. His manner was polite to those he passed, friendly but official. Everyone bowed to him.

"I want to be like you when I grow up," I had told him.

He had smiled.

"Good. You're learning how to obey and be a good citizen."

MY SCHOOL, A LONG CONCRETE BUILDING, WAS CO-ED AND for students between the ages of seven and eleven. We always began our day with a bow and by listening to stories about our eternal leader, Kim Il-sung. My favorite was the *Learning Journey of a Thousand Miles*. It's about our eternal leader as a small child, living in exile with his family in Manchuria. When he was about ten, Kim Il-sung was sent by his father back to his Joseon hometown, Mangyeongdae. Our eternal leader had to journey alone and was given no food and no clothing other than what he wore on his back. Traversing winter storms, mountains covered in ice, and jagged crags, and encountering attacking falcons and hawks and predators, including tigers, he passed through many valleys full of death. He made it safely to Mangyeongdae, mostly because of the help of strangers, other Koreans.

After storytelling, we would quote sayings from our eternal leader and occasionally from Kim Jong-il. "The first priority for students is to study hard," our class would call out in a loud voice, standing up, our backs straight, our eyes glued to the wall in front of us. "We must give our all in the struggle to unify the entire society with the revolutionary ideology of the Great Leader Kim Il-sung. We must learn from the Great Leader Comrade Kim Il-sung and adopt the communist look, revolutionary work methods, and people-oriented work style."

History—or what I now call propaganda—was often the first, fourth, and final subject of the day, and the lessons almost always began with the same introduction.

NORTH KOREA WAS FOUNDED IN 1948 AFTER A LONG BAT-tle between our Japanese oppressors and the liberation army of Kim Il-sung. Our fearless leader braved battles with no food, in the chill of deep winter, walking thousands of miles to lead his armies to rid this land of the foreigners who had taken our natural resources for themselves and turned our people into slaves. Our eternal leader made rice from sand on the shores of the Duman and Amnok rivers to feed his armies and turned pinecones into grenades when his armies were weaponless . . .

WOW! THIS MAN WAS, OF COURSE, MY IDOL! I WANTED TO be brave and magical, just like him. He was everyone's idol.

When I was a small child, my mother told me the Myth of Dangun. Dangun is said to be the grandson of heaven. His story began when his father, Hwanung, wanted to live on earth. Hwanung fell to Baekdu Mountain, where he built a city in which, aided by heavenly forces, humans advanced in the arts, sciences, and farming.

A tiger and a bear told Hwanung that they wanted to be human, too. Hwanung ordered them to eat only cloves of garlic and mugwort for one hundred days. The tiger gave up, but the bear pressed on. When the bear became human, she was pregnant and husbandless. Hwanung married her. The bear's son, Dangun, became the leader of the heavenly kingdom on earth and moved the capital to outside Pyongyang.

In my imagination, Kim Il-sung was a descendant of Dangun. He was part god, too.

After history, we moved on to geometry, biology, algebra, dance and music, the last of which I hated, for I felt these were subjects for girls.

After school, I would go to tae kwon do lessons at the most rigorous *sojo* in all of Pyongyang. "It's where the boys who will become military leaders start their training," my father told me each and every time he came to watch me do my tae kwon do patterns.

My mother would look away whenever my father talked of my plans to be in the military because she didn't want me to become a career soldier. She once told me that my father was never home and that she didn't want my future wife to feel the heaviness she did in her own heart whenever he was away. Her eyes drooped at the sides, reminding me of a doe I had once seen at the petting zoo at the amusement park Mangyeongdae Yuheejang. Mother's irises were a soft brown, like the coat of a meadow bunting, and her speech was like a love song I might hear on my father's radio.

My mother performed the traditional fan dance. I saw her do it only once, when I was nine, at the home of my paternal grandfather. She circled the room in the traditional dress of a white skirt with a red top and a long gold ribbon that stretched from her chest to the floor. She also wore a headdress that matched the gold and red in the fans she made float around the room like the wings of a swift. On a nearby stereo, someone had put on a record of flute and *gayageum* music.

My mother reminded me of midsummer sunsets.

MY BIRTHDAY IS IN MARCH. I WON'T TELL YOU THE EXACT Western year and month or the year by the Juche calendar we use in North Korea, the first year of which is 1912, when Kim Il-sung was born. But I can tell you that my birthday falls about a month before the biggest celebration of all in North Korea: our eternal father's own birthday, April 15, also known as the Day of the Sun. On this day, every year, lots of stories were published in the newspapers about our supreme leader's childhood.

On my birthday, I had all my friends to my apartment—friends from school and friends from the tae kwon do *sojo*. My birthday meal, like that of most boys in Pyongyang, was always eggs and pork, both of which represented, my mother would tell us as she passed around our bowls, "prosperity and good fortune."

I'd always end my birthday by playing in the park, even if the ground was still covered in snow. My friends and I would reenact war battles, and I was the general of the Joseon army. I'd go first, picking one boy to be part of my unit. Another boy would be leader of the American imperialists. He'd pick next, and then me again, and so on until all the boys were chosen. We'd then hunt each other down, using sticks as guns. If my unit caught a member of the opposing army, we'd lock him up in the makeshift prison of the twisted iron of the jungle gym. My side, naturally, always won, as we represented the greatest country on earth. Then my unit would march, with me leading it, as in my dream, past my father, whom I would salute, as if he were our great eternal father standing on a platform in the center of Kim Il-sung Square.

ost people in the United States remember where they were on September 11, 2001. For people in Joseon, the day everyone remembers is July 8, 1994, or year 82 in the Juche calendar.

It was a Friday. I came home from school to find our apartment empty. My mother was still at her job as a teacher.

I stretched out on the floor underneath the baby grand piano and played with my toy soldiers. Because it was a regular school day, there were no television signals and so I couldn't watch *Boy General*. I was bored.

While I was very much content fulfilling my obligations as a child to attain the goal of being a military leader, the truth was that I was also lonely. I was going for my white belt in tae kwon do and practicing every second day. I was also studying at the top elementary school to gain entrance to an engineering program at the university, as my father said that being

an engineer meant I could help the reg.

tunnels for our armies to hide in, for instance

child. I wanted a sibling, a brother. And so, in quiet .

then, when only the tick-tock of the clock in the foyer

heard, a loneliness grew out of me like a rose aching to bloom.

On this day, I was particularly sad because some of my friends had planned during the August school break to visit the sea. I'd never been, but wanted to. My father's work kept him in Pyong-yang, and, therefore, my mother and I weren't going anywhere—like every other August holiday.

Then I heard it. A song? No, a wail, followed by another, and soon several voices were crying, almost howling, in unison.

I pushed myself up against the wall, my entire body shaking. Dread filled me. "We've been invaded," I whispered out loud, tossing my army figurines onto the floor.

"*Eomeoni!*" I called out, hoping maybe, just maybe, she was somewhere in the apartment. Silence, at least inside. Outside, the noise grew louder.

I pulled myself up and out from underneath the piano and crept to the window. As I neared, my heart started to beat wildly, as if my insides already knew something that my eyes were just getting ready to see. I reached up to open the window and discovered my hands were shaking.

"*Eomeoni*," I stammered, hearing the latch of the door. "You o come!" I was unable to look away from the scene below

"*Adeul*," my mother called out, her feet a soft pitter-patter on the hardwood floor that was protected by a mustard-colored sheet of paper.

She pulled me into her arms and held me tight around the waist. "*Adeul*, we haven't been invaded," she whispered in my ear. "Something else has happened. The eternal leader has died."

I looked up. Her eyes were red, and tears dripped down her cheeks and stained her white silk blouse.

"*Eomeoni*," I said, choking on my words.

My mother fell to the floor then, with me still in her arms. We remained huddled together like this, so lost in some mist that we didn't even get up to bow to my father when he arrived home. All I remember is *abeoji* sliding to the ground, joining us, too.

MY MOTHER'S PARENTS—MY GRANDFATHER, *HAL-ABEOJI*, and my grandmother, *hal-meoni*—found the three of us in this position when twilight pulled itself over the city.

My mother's father was a doctor and had a busy practice, so I never saw him much. I didn't recognize him at first because his hair was thinning and graying at the temples and the lines on his face had deepened. But he had the same droop in the corners of his eyes as my mother and the bushiest eyebrows of anyone I had ever met. My grandmother carried a basket of white magnolias, which she said we would offer as a family at the foot of the statue of our supreme leader on Mansudae Hill. "To show how grateful we all are for the abundance our eternal father has shown us," she whispered.

I tried to eat some kimchi and pork with *abeoji* and my grandfather, but not much made it to my stomach. I picked at the food with my chopsticks and looked down into my bowl the entire time. My mother had opened the windows wide so we could share in the mourning, which came in big waves, as I imagined the sea would do against a rugged, sharp shoreline. Inside, we were all quiet, like the family of mice I had once stumbled upon nesting in a tiny hole where the wall ended and the floor in the hallway of our apartment building began.

That night, we went as a family to the monument. Walking, we melted into the crowd, shuffling our feet and moving so slowly that crawling on all fours would have got us to Mansudae Hill faster. We were in a sea of bodies, crying and swaying from side to side on the heels of their shoes as if the world itself had ended. When it was finally my family's turn to lay down the white magnolias and show our respect, my father bowed three times and then wailed like all the others, shocking me, for I'd never seen him cry before. As I started to move toward the monument, my mother pulled me back. Red-faced and perspiring from the heat of so many people, she pinched my arm hard and ordered me to cry, too.

"But I can't," I said in such a low voice even she couldn't hear. "I thought Kim Il-sung was a god. Gods don't die."

WHEN WE GOT HOME, I WAS SENT RIGHT TO BED. BUT I tossed and turned on my mat in my room, listening to the wailing outside, which eventually retreated, like a swarm of bees following their queen to a new home, until our apartment was silent again . . . except for the tick-tock of the clock and the chime announcing the coming of the hour . . . *one, two* . . . *three*—that's when I pulled myself up and crept to the front door.

Unlike other times when I snuck out to be with Bo-Cho, on this night my feet moved as if I were wearing socks made of lead. I kept thinking that when I stepped outside I would meet the spirit of our eternal leader, and he would be cross with me for not crying. For the first time, I was also conscious that my nights with Bo-Cho did not make me a good son of the government. But I was more lonely than afraid, so I pushed on, tiptoeing down the concrete staircase.

Just as I pushed open the side door to our apartment building and felt the warm night air embrace me, a strong hand grabbed the collar of my shirt and pulled me through. I pinched my eyes shut, convinced I was about to face the ghost of the eternal leader.

"Open your eyes, my little *yaeya*," a familiar voice said.

I looked into my grandfather's wrinkled face, lit by the match he was using to light a cigarette.

My legs shook. Boys I knew, when they did something wrong, got beatings from their fathers. I was sure that was coming my way. Adding to my fears was my grandfather's cold stare as he puffed on his cigarette in silence.

"Where are you going?" he finally asked, putting out his cigarette and taking another from his shirt pocket. His voice was thick and smooth, like honey, which I'd only ever had with my grandfather. "Honey's very hard to get," he had told me as he dipped a spoon into the syrupy, sweet liquid and then poured it into some hot water. "My dream"—he had winked—"is to one day look after the bees that make the honey."

I was defeated. I didn't want to lie to my grandfather. I'd face my punishment. "To see Bo-Cho," I said after a long pause and with a sigh. "I'm going to see Bo-Cho."

My grandfather's laugh was first low and then rose, eventually erupting like a volcano, scaring me with its force, for I thought for sure he was going to awaken the entire building.

Then he stopped, put a finger to his lips, and said, "Shush," as if I were the one making all the noise, not him. "Show me what you do when you sneak out at night," he said.

I nodded nervously and pointed with a shaking hand at Bo-Cho's home.

"Do you just stand there and look at it?" my grandfather asked.

"No," I admitted, digging a toe into the ground. "I usually . . . ," I started and then stopped. "I'm embarrassed to say."

"You usually what?" he probed.

"I usually go inside," I said with another sigh.

"Inside what?" he asked, startling me because he ended his question with a laugh. In history class, I had learned that the best way to get political prisoners to reveal their secrets was to make them laugh and trust their interrogators. I couldn't tell whether my grandfather was goading me, getting me to admit to him what I did at night so he could decide the best way to punish me.

"Inside what?" he asked again, cocking an eyebrow.

I groaned. "I usually go inside Bo-Cho's house and lie beside him." I then got down on my knees, lowered my head, and started to plead with him to have mercy on me. "I'm only a child, only a decade old. I'm sorry I made such a mistake not crying over our eternal father's death and by sneaking out to be with Bo-Cho."

My grandfather's fingers spread out on top of my head like an octopus's tentacles. "I'm not angry," he whispered, tilting my head up so I had to look right at him. For once, he was not smoking. "Let's go in together," he said. "Do you think we'll both fit?"

It was a tight squeeze, but somehow the three of us managed to lie down, with our heads outside the door. Bo-Cho rested his head of soft, short fur on my chest while my grandfather and I looked up at the stars. For a while, we remained quiet, listening to the crickets. Then my grandfather asked if I wanted to hear a story.

"Yes, *hal-abeoji*," I said, beaming. I sure did.

"THERE WERE ONCE TWO BROTHERS, HEUNGBU AND NOLBU. Nolbu was very greedy, whereas Heungbu was compassionate and kind. When their father died, the boys were told to split their father's fortune in two. But Nolbu refused. He took it all, and Heungbu and his family became very poor.

"One day a snake was climbing up a tree near Heungbu's house, wanting to eat a swallow. Heungbu chased the snake away and helped the swallow heal from its injuries. The swallow's family gave Heungbu a seed as a thank-you. That seed grew into gourds that, when opened, were full of jewels that brought Heungbu and his family great wealth.

"On hearing of Heungbu's good fortune, Nolbu wanted a gourd, too. So he broke a swallow's leg and then fixed it, hoping the swallow would repay the kindness with a magic seed. But when Nolbu split open his gourds, great pain came out, leaving his family now very poor."

"THE MORAL OF THE STORY," MY GRANDFATHER TOLD ME, stroking my forehead in much the same way my mother did when I had a fever, "is that good deeds lay a foundation for a house of great wealth and luck. Greed and ego, however, lay a foundation of destruction. The house that is built on such a foundation, one day, no matter what, will be torn down."

A dark blanket pulled itself over Pyongyang, a blanket that hugged us tight from the day our eternal leader died until . . . well, two and a half years later. People talked in whispers on the streets when they moved from work to home. In our house, *abeoji* was always tired. He no longer tutored me in math or lectured me to practice more tae kwon do or to study harder. It was as though he no longer cared if I did well or not. My mother said that part of mourning was being quiet and sad. It was our way, she said, of honoring the loss of our eternal leader.

I believed her at first and thought this was why the people on the streets looked like deflating balloons as they drooped down from the sky after the Day of the Sun. But as the creases on my mother's forehead darkened and she stopped playing the piano,

I began to wonder if something else was going on that she and *abeoji* weren't telling me.

I felt emptier than I ever had.

IT WAS A SCHOOL DAY IN JANUARY 1997, ABOUT TWO months before my tenth birthday. I was returning from the tae kwon do *sojo*, walking home on a sidewalk layered with an icing of powdered snow. I held my mouth open, catching snowflakes on my tongue. As I approached my apartment building, two things happened that were omens that my life was about to take a drastic turn—for the worse.

The first: Just as I passed under the streetlamp, the light flickered and then went out. The second was when I discovered a bird of prey, a falcon or a hawk, dead on the walkway, its white stomach held high, as if it were a king, even in its afterlife. I didn't have to step through our door and be engulfed in the thick air of sadness to know. Seeing *eomeoni*'s tear-streaked face, with *abeoji* behind her, shaking his head and rocking back and forth on his heels, repeating, "No, no, no," I burst into tears and fell to my knees. Had the school called and said I failed an examination? Had I not graded well enough to receive my first belt in tae kwon do? Had someone else died? "Have I failed you, *abeoji*?" I cried in despair.

My mother pulled me into her arms and rubbed my back. "We're going on a long vacation," she whispered. "Your father . . ."

"My father what?"

"Your father has been asked to go away for a while . . . to take a holiday," *eomeoni* said, squeezing me so tight, it hurt.

"Why?" I said, pulling myself loose.

"Because America is blocking our imports and exports. America threatens our most peaceful land." Her voice was wavering, so she paused and cleared her throat. "We're going on a long vacation," she then repeated. She tried to smile to reassure me.

"I don't understand," I said, staring at her, so many thoughts flooding my head I didn't know which question to ask first. "If America is threatening us, we need to be *here*," I finally said. My father and I would be needed to help defend the country.

"We're going on a holiday to the north . . . near the sea," my father said in a hoarse voice. I turned to him. He was wearing his work clothes from the day before, including a khaki wool Mao jacket that was rumpled, as if he'd slept in it.

"What should I do?" I asked in a desperate voice, looking back to my mother. Her soft brown eyes wilted at the corners, like a rose just past full bloom.

"I'll bring you a chest to put your clothes in."

"And my books and comics?"

My father coughed. I looked over. He shook his head.

"You can't take everything," my mother whispered. "There won't be room. I'll help you choose what you can bring."

My father moved in beside *eomeoni*. "You'll be going to a new school while we're on holiday," he said.

I just stared at him. I didn't even blink. I wanted him to answer my question about why we were leaving when we were needed here, but in Joseon, a son never demands explanations from his elders. I had to wait.

"And Bo-Cho?" I asked instead.

My father looked down and bit his lip as if he were trying not to weep.

"Who will look after him?" I cried out.

"Someone will," he said.

I turned quickly and ran to the front door, my father not far behind me, calling my name and telling me to stop. But I didn't stop until I was outside, where I saw one of my father's colleagues leading Bo-Cho away on a leash.

I willed my feet to move faster than they've ever moved in my life.

I chased after the man, but as I turned a corner, I ran right into a lady pushing a baby in a pram. I landed on the hard concrete with a thud. I lay on the ground wailing, as my mother had wanted me to do when Kim Il-sung died, blood from my wounds reddening the snow underneath me, people and more snow collecting around me.

A week later we headed to the train station for our so-called northern holiday. My father and I plopped our bags down on the platform, as well as the oak wedding chest that had been made especially for my mother to take new linens, fine china, and silverware from her parents' house to *abeoji*'s when they married. My mother gripped my hand hard, and we stood off to the side as we watched my father hand a policeman our papers giving us permission to travel. The papers said that we were going to a city called Gyeong-seong and that, while on vacation, my parents would serve the country by working as laborers.

The police officer ran his eyes up and down my father and then turned and did the same to my mother and me. *Eomeoni* blushed and looked down. I stood up straight, as if I were about to salute the man. The policeman huffed some words to my father, passed the papers back, and then stomped off.

As my father and I heaved the chest toward the edge of the platform to wait for the train, my eyes landed on the policeman, who had stopped to talk to some colleagues. They were all looking at my father, with expressions on their faces that sent a shiver through me. I'd seen that look before, on my classmates' faces when we talked about the Japanese colonialists and the evil Americans. It was that look that said "We're better than you."

ON THE TRAIN, MY FATHER LEANED BACK IN HIS SEAT AND closed his eyes. I sensed he wanted to escape as much as I did. I opened my sketchbook and, with the one pencil that my mother had said I could take with me, drew a BTR-40, also known as a Bronetransporter tank, which the Soviet Union built and our armies used in the 1950s to try to free the South from American control.

After a while, the constant sway of the train made me dizzy, so I closed my eyes like *abeoji*. The clickety-clack sound of the train lulled me into a fitful sleep in which I felt my muscles twitch. I dreamed I was at Mangyeongdae Yuheejang. I saw myself on the Ferris wheel, looking down at the purple and white lilac blossoms and at *abeoji* and *eomeoni* smiling and waving. I heard music from the nearby merry-go-round. I felt light and carefree, knowing that when I got off my ride, I would be enjoying a drink of sweet water.

I woke up with a jolt, perspiring and breathing heavily. I looked over at *abeoji* and *eomeoni*, who were both asleep. I caught my breath and then brushed my messy hair using some spit and the palms of my hands. I closed my sketchbook, tucked the pencil into my shirt pocket, and looked out the window.

I wished I hadn't.

The train was starting to slow, its brakes screeching us to a halt. Our carriage eventually stopped with the window facing the end of the platform. I leaned my face up to the window, so close my breath caused it to steam. I wiped the window clean and then looked out. Lines of people stretched out before me, but people unlike any I'd seen in Pyongyang. Their skin sagged, their eyes were sinking into their faces, and their complexions were bluish, almost gray, like the clouds that rolled off the East Sea in February. The men didn't wear Mao jackets but dirty dark gray or blue pants and matching tops. The women weren't in skirts, nor did they wear their hair neat on top of their heads in buns. They also wore pants and jackets, and their hair was messy. Some of the children wore shoes with big holes in them through which I could see their toes. These children's faces were covered in scabs and a white coating, like patches of snow on the grasses of the parks in early spring.

Like the barricades that kept spectators off the roads on parade days, policemen blocked the steps up to the train. Some people were slipping won, North Korean currency, to the policemen along with their papers that looked, at a distance, like ours. The policemen wouldn't take the documents, though. They shook their heads, their facial expressions cold, their gaze looking out beyond the train station, over to some sloping mountains.

People fell to their knees, wailing . . . *wailing,* as if our eternal leader had passed away a second time. I could make out some of the words they shouted to the policemen: "Please, I need to see a dying relative! . . . Please, my children are starving and waiting for me! . . . Please let me on the train!"

Tears flowed down the wrinkled cheeks of an old woman who had managed to push her way to the front using her pointy elbows. Some of her gray hair was missing, exposing red-chaffed skin on her scalp. The policeman in front of our carriage, a stiff young man, tossed the papers she tried to give him into the air like confetti. The old woman crumpled to the platform as if she were lying down for a nap. The crowd moved in on top of her.

The day that started off sunny and winter-crisp turned cloudy. As we moved north, sleet slapped at the windowpanes.

I was glad for that, for I couldn't see out the window anymore.

INSIDE THE GYEONG-SEONG TRAIN STATION, I BECAME very aware of my clean clothes and clean body amid all the dirty faces and the dirty floor and walls, which I took to have once been white but were now covered with a dull yellow film. I shifted uncomfortably from foot to foot under the gaze of the people, who must have noticed, too. I stood out, I thought, like *eomeoni*'s gold wedding band on a black piece of fabric.

I shifted my eyes to my father as he approached a young man, about the same age as me, standing in the center of the room. The boy was singing the "Spring of Hometown." His shrill voice moved around the room like a warm summer wind and made me smile for the first time that day.

Still singing, the boy turned his head to listen to something my father asked him. He pointed to another boy standing nearby. This boy was small, with red eyes that circled the room, like the singer's voice. He was bone-thin, like a newly planted cherry tree, and his hair was bushy, wild, and dull-looking, not short and shiny like the hair of the boys in Pyongyang. My father spoke to him and then waved for *eomeoni* and me to come.

Once outside, the boy grabbed hold of my mother's wedding chest and, despite his frail appearance, hoisted it without any help onto the back of a pull-cart. My father handed him our papers and some won, and we followed on foot as he wheeled the cart away from the station and through the town. The only light was from tiny lamps set in the windowsills of the houses, which were wooden and small. There were no apartment buildings. But there was a mural in the middle of town with a saying from Kim Il-sung underneath it. In the dim light, I couldn't read it, though.

I listened to the soles of my mother's loafers crunch the snow. I lowered my head and watched my feet as snowflakes drifted down around me like cherry blossoms falling in Pyongyang's Daedong River. Tonight I didn't want to try to catch them in my mouth.

Tonight the snowflakes reminded me of large pieces of dust that collect in the corners of rooms and underneath furniture.

THE PULL-CART DRIVER TOOK US TO THE PARTY OFFICIAL who was responsible for overseeing Gyeong-seong. This man was thin, too, like the boy, with stubble on his face and slits for eyes. He had my mother and me sit in an outer room beside a wood-burning heater while he and my father talked behind a closed door. When my father emerged, his face was red, and he looked weary, as if he were losing a military battle but wasn't quite ready to surrender. *Eomeoni* went to him and touched his shoulder. Over the years, he and my mother had become like one, moving as if a symphony played between them. I had, at times, studied their unspoken language, and I knew my mother was now asking if everything was fine. *Abeoji*, stone-faced, waved her away.

No, I thought, *nothing is fine*.

We headed back into the cold, *eomeoni* and me following the cart while *abeoji* walked in front, beside the boy. We finally stopped by a dark gray house with a door painted royal blue. I dropped the bags I was carrying and ran, pushing open the door, which wasn't locked. I flipped on the light switch. It didn't work. *Eomeoni* rushed past me and with some matches she carried in her purse lit one of two kerosene lamps placed in the middle of the floor. I looked around. Paint was peeling from the walls, and in some places the walls weren't even painted—just bare concrete. The front room was a kitchen, with three black iron pots sitting on the woodstove. There was a sink, with tubes coming from it and leading to the outside. "Our vacation home!" *abeoji* said, faking a smile. He then patted me on the back. "A little smaller than our apartment in Pyongyang, but it's only for a short while."

"I was hoping this was my new dog's home," I said, sighing.

"*Adeul*," my father began. "I'm sorry. You'll get used to the small size. I know it."

I inspected the room off the kitchen. The lamps that my mother lit, while dim, still revealed all the house's dirt, and its yellow walls—like the train station and the oil—and the foot stains on the paper flooring. It felt like an old home, a dying home.

I turned and asked my father, "Why did we really leave Pyongyang?"

MY FATHER AND I SAT CROSS-LEGGED ON THE GROUND, watching *eomeoni* put wood in the stove and boil water that she had pumped in through those long tubes that led, she explained, to an outside well. In Pyongyang, we had faucets and pipes that were connected to the city's water and sewage system. "Here we have an outhouse for a toilet," she explained. "When you have to go, I'll show you where."

My father cleared his throat. "I want to answer your question about why we left Pyongyang as best I can," he said. "What you're learning in school isn't everything there is to know about Joseon," he continued slowly, as if thinking hard about every word. "There are problems . . . The country is facing problems. Here in the countryside"—he waved his hand around the room as if all of it represented rural Joseon—"life is different. I mean, Pyongyang's great monuments, museums, hotels, and theaters were all built in the 1960s and 1970s—everything is new and efficient. Here . . . well, here all the buildings owned by the Japanese were destroyed, but those built in their place are not as state-of-the-art as in Pyongyang. It will be a hard vacation, but one designed to test your strength and open your eyes to how the rest of the country lives."

I didn't say anything, but with every word my father spoke, my shoulders slumped a little more. "*Abeoji*, are we really on vacation?" I eventually asked, looking deep into my father's eyes. But then, as I studied his eyes, which were the color of varnished oak, I felt guilty. *A good son trusts his parents*, I lectured myself. My shoulders slackened again, and my head drooped. I had betrayed my father and my role as his son by even hinting that I didn't believe him.

"We're on holiday," he repeated, tilting my head up with his hand and forcing me to look at him.

Eomeoni sat down with a sigh. "Look, *adeul*," she started, "Joseon is facing some problems."

Okay. I had heard that. "What kind of problems?" I asked.

"I can't fully say, but it's all due to the evil Americans," she said.

I bowed to show I agreed. But I didn't understand. I wasn't getting enough information to understand. At least in school when the teacher says the Japanese did terrible things, the teacher also lists everything the Japanese did when they occupied our land.

"Look at this holiday as a test, a test of your courage," *abeoji* repeated.

"And strength to lead an army one day," *eomeoni* added.

I looked at her with surprise. It was the first time she had ever acknowledged my future dreams to be a military leader.

"Like when our eternal leader set off on foot from Manchuria to Mangyeongdae?" I whispered to her. "The *Learning Journey of a Thousand Miles*?"

She nodded. "Yes, *adeul*. Like that time."

5

awoke early the next day. I sat up quickly and looked over to the window. Dirt filtered the sunlight that was trying to stretch itself into the one room where we now all slept side by side on the floor.

Still in that fog between wake and sleep, I crept out from underneath my covers and crossed the icy-cold floor. Our vacation house had no central heating, unlike our apartment in Pyongyang. Now only the stove in the main room warmed us. Like the sun, the stove's warmth also struggled to spread itself into the house. I could see my breath steaming up the air.

The lower part of the inside of the window was covered in a thin layer of ice. Using a fingernail, I chipped at it, creating a small pile of snow powder on the floor and a clear patch of window, which I could peer through. *Snow*—all I could see was white snow that sparkled like jewels in the sunlight.

My father and I ate a bowl of noodles and broth in silence,

partly because I was still ashamed of myself for questioning him the day before. Also, I was freezing. My teeth chattered and my fingers shook when I lifted my bowl to my lips.

"I have a trick for you," my father finally said.

I smiled. I liked tricks.

"In the army, when men are sent out for long marches and it's cold like this and they're hungry, we get them to play a game in which they think about their favorite foods and eating these foods in the warmest places they know. Can you do that?"

"Yes," I said, closing my eyes. My mind drifted to my birthday: tender pork in a special sauce that *eomeoni* alone in this world knew how to make, hard-boiled eggs, and steamed bread with red bean paste. "Nampo's wedding!" I then shouted. "Remember, *abeoji*? Aunt Nampo's wedding?"

I heard him say, "Uh-huh."

"Sugar candies shaped like flowers," I continued. "I ate a yellow tulip and a peach rose. It was summer, and we wore short-sleeved shirts. I was warm . . ."

I then thought of a long, hot bath.

It worked.

My father was right.

When I opened my eyes, I felt full and warm. I pulled myself up and changed into a pair of slacks, with tights underneath to keep the chill out. I then headed with my father to my new school.

¤ ¤ ¤

MY FATHER SAT IN A STIFF FOLDING WOODEN CHAIR FAC-
ing the principal's long wooden desk. The principal appeared
small sitting behind a mound of Kim Il-sung books and swimming in an oversize thick woolen coat, which I wondered why he
wore, given his tininess. He looked at us through lost gray eyes,
the color of which matched his salt-and-pepper hair. He didn't
wear a Mao suit, like the principal at my school in Pyongyang, and
he spoke with an accent that I found hard to understand at first. It
was rough, like the barking of a large dog.

The *so-nyon-dan* manager came in and introduced himself.
He explained to my father that, like the *so-nyon-dan* manager in
Pyongyang, he taught the anti-imperialist courses and oversaw
biweekly revealing sessions, in which the class lists the things
they had not done right. Back in Pyongyang, my answer was almost always that I had skipped studying to watch *Boy General*.
In these sessions, we also had to condemn our peers for what
they did wrong. The goal was to help us become good citizens, of
course, and follow the rules of the country, the *so-nyon-dan* manager explained to my father, as if we didn't know this already. "If
we reveal our problems and point out to others where they need
to improve, we won't repeat the wrongs in the future," he said. I
could tell he was trying to impress my father. At least he wasn't
acting like the policemen at the Pyongyang train station.

Then the *so-nyon-dan* manager told me to follow him to my
new classroom. "We will be having an election to decide the stu-

dent council president soon," he said as we trudged back through the snow, past some low buildings that he waved a hand toward and said were other classrooms. "I'm sure you know from your schooling in Pyongyang that part of our education is to learn to agree with the decisions made by those in authority. We've discussed it and decided that, because you are from Pyongyang and attended such a distinguished school before coming here, we would like you to be the student council president."

I bowed to show that I agreed. I knew that my elite upbringing destined me to be a leader. Part of my education was to accept my responsibility.

He led me onto a cobblestone path that had recently been shoveled. We followed it as it wove around several more low wooden buildings, which I figured were outhouses. Finally, the *so-nyon-dan* manager stopped in front of a building that he said was my new classroom. He led me inside. With me standing nervously behind him, he introduced me to the students.

The room had no electricity, but there was a long window that let in lots of light. The room was heated, I could see, by a small wood-burning stove in the corner. I shivered, and not just from the cold. All the students were staring at me with shocked expressions.

In Pyongyang, my classmates had always been the same since I was seven. No one ever left, until, well, me, and no new students ever came. I guessed it must be the same up here. My face suddenly felt flushed, and I wrung my hands together.

The teacher, who asked me to call him *seon-saeng-nim*, or simply "teacher," moved a student from the front of the class to the back. "You're from Pyongyang," he said to me. I was getting that this fact alone granted me privileges the others didn't have, including sitting close to him. I wasn't so sure I wanted to, though. His body odor filled the room, and he spoke in a harsh, gruff voice that, when he recited Kim Il-sung sayings, pounded at my ears like a *buk*. This man, too, swam in his suits. I looked down and saw that his shoes were large, like flippers a military diver wears. I shrugged. Maybe men in the countryside just like wearing clothes that are too big for them.

I WAS QUICKER THAN ANY OF MY CLASSMATES IN SOLVING geometry questions, so I made a mental note at afternoon break to ask my father if I could move to a higher class.

As I reached under my desk to pull out the container of noodles my mother had given me for a snack, a strong hand grabbed my elbow. I looked up quickly into the round black eyes of another boy. "I'm Young-bum," he chirped like a bird. His hair was short and choppy, as if he had cut it himself with dull scissors and without a mirror.

I nodded back. Like his eyes, Young-bum had a round, glowing face. He also had high cheekbones. He was tall—that much I could see, as his legs spread out underneath his desk like tree roots. He had long fingers, and when he caught me looking at them, he informed me with a big grin that he played the accordion. "I'm also the best fighter in the school," he boasted. "So what's it like in Pyongyang? Have you been to Mangyeongdae Yuheejang?" He ran his tongue over the name of the amusement park as if he were hungry. "Did you ride the Ferris wheel?"

"Yes," I replied, sadly remembering the amusement park. I felt as if I were sinking. I wanted to go home.

"What was it like?"

"Fun," I replied.

I studied Young-bum. He was peppy, like Bo-Cho when he saw me rounding the corner on my way home from school. Young-bum was unable to keep still in his chair, tapping his foot and moving around, like some red candy *abeoji* once gave me that popped when I put it in my mouth. "What's the name of the amusement park here?" I finally asked.

"We don't have amusement parks," another boy said. He plopped himself down on the edge of Young-bum's desk and introduced himself as Chulho. I gasped and tried hard not to show my dismay. Boys in Pyongyang would never be this informal.

"Umm . . . ," I started, turning my attention from Young-bum to Chulho. Everything about him seemed sharp, from his pointy nose and lips, which were like two longs sticks, to his eyebrows, which looked like the mustache my father painted on my general figurine. His lanky body reminded me of a flagpole.

"We have nothing in Gyeong-seong," he spat out with such force that his tone of voice was like an acid I once used for an experiment in science class. "But you in Pyongyang are rich and get good food and Ferris wheels."

"Don't forget roller coasters and swimming pools," Young-bum said, bouncing in his seat. These two couldn't have been more opposite, I thought. Like sweet-and-sour sauce my father brought home once, saying it was a gift from a man who traded Joseon goods in China.

Suddenly a boy sitting behind Chulho caught my attention.

"I know him," I said, pointing. "But I can't remember . . ."

"Oh," Young-bum said, turning. "That's Sangchul."

"For the past three years, he's won the regional singing competition performing '*So-nian-jang-soo*,'" Chulho jumped in. "He's a singer."

"You probably saw him at the train station," Young-bum added.

"Yeah, that's Sangchul, all right," Chulho continued. "He goes there to sing, to make won for his family."

I tilted my head and blinked. "What?" I asked in disbelief.

"Sangchul can earn more won than anyone in his family—well, more than any of us put together—with his singing," Young-bum said, beaming.

I shook my head. "I don't understand," I said. "I mean, what does he need won for? The government provides for everything, and surely if his family wants extra, they're earning won at their places of work."

Chulho's laughter drowned out my words. "There are no rations here," he finally said, folding his arms across his chest. "Surely you know that. The government isn't providing for anything anymore."

"I . . . I . . ." I was stammering now.

"Look," said Chulho, leaning toward me and opening a brown bag. He then motioned for me to take a look inside. All I could see were strips of some kind of reddish meat covered in crystals of gray salt. I shrugged, trying to act cool, as if I knew what was going on. But I sure didn't.

"It's squirrel meat. I caught a squirrel in the forests last fall," he said.

"Okay," I said, playing along.

He cocked an eyebrow. "It's all I'm going to eat today?" he said, the end of his sentence rising as if it were a question instead of a statement.

A laugh spilled out of me now. For sure, Chulho was playing with me. No one ate squirrel.

The room fell silent, and so did I. I slowly looked around and saw that every eye was on me again. I swallowed hard and chewed the inside of my mouth.

"What were you told about your move to Gyeong-seong?" Chulho asked as Young-bum pulled his chair up beside mine and stuck his big head close to me.

I wiped my sweaty forehead with the sleeve of my shirt. I remembered the mock interrogations we would do in class in Pyongyang. This felt like one of those times—but different. I wasn't sure if this interrogation was real or not.

I took a deep breath and kept looking down. I refused to answer, which was what I was told most prisoners of war do, at least at first, before the torture starts.

"I don't know what you were told, but I'll tell you the truth," Chulho said, leaning in close, too, so close I could smell that he smoked, which startled me. Children don't smoke in Pyongyang, only adults. "The factories up here may be open, yet no one is working in them, because what's the point?" he said. "People don't get paid won for the hours they put in. The food-distribution centers are empty, so their ration tickets are useless. There's no hope here, fancy-pants Pyongyang boy."

Nervous perspiration dripped down my forehead, making my eyes itch. I wished—I wished so much—that *seon-saeng-nim* would return from his break and start lessons again.

"Soon *you'll* be out in those forests looking for food," Young-bum said more gently. "And when you do, I'll come with you. It won't be that scary."

At that moment, *seon-saeng-nim* burst through the front door, sending a blast of cold air around the already cold room. I exhaled, never so happy in my life to see a teacher.

As *seon-saeng-nim* went on about Japan's expansion into Joseon over the 1900s, Chulho passed me a note.

Trust me, those yummy noodles you just ate will soon run out. Then you'll be just like us.

wasn't allowed to switch classes to be exposed to a harder curriculum. For one, this class was apparently the most difficult in the school and had the top students, which I found hard to believe. My father said he would discuss with our block party leader if there were some activities I could do outside of school to further my studies. In the meantime, I stayed away from these Young-bum and Chulho characters, reading my textbooks during breaks and running right home from school at lunch and at the end of the day. I was sure the boys were not serious about what they had said to me. Yet why would they lie? Was it to test me? To see if I was strong and would continue to support the regime under interrogation?

While I waited for *eomeoni* to return from her job on a government farm, I collected wood and twigs for the fire, and water, in a large metal bucket, from the well. I had food every day, good food, from sticky rice with kidney beans and vegetables to fried tofu and kimchi. Life up here was just fine, I thought on some days, although I missed watching *Boy General* on television because we didn't have a TV. Even if we did, the electricity was turned on only for special occasions. I missed Bo-Cho and my *sojo*. *Our eternal father sacrificed much more than I am*, I reminded myself when I felt sad. *This is all a test of my willpower, and I will be strong.*

Spring soon came. The hills and fields became dotted with red and yellow azaleas, and geese called out to me from above, announcing that they were on their way home from their own winter vacations.

Just before biology class a few weeks after Kim Il-sung's birthday, Young-bum skidded his chair and jumpy body beside mine and whispered, "We're going to an execution tomorrow."

I stared at him for the longest time, not sure if I had heard him correctly. I wondered if he was just testing me again.

"A what?" I finally asked, deciding I'd feign that I hadn't quite made out what he'd said.

"An execution. Where the government kills people." Chulho joined us, squeezing his thin frame in between Young-bum's and mine. "Don't tell me you proper people in Pyongyang don't execute people who commit crimes?"

"No!" I wanted to shout out at him. But I didn't. I said nothing.

"Or maybe no one in Pyongyang does anything wrong?" Young-bum interrupted, cocking his head and smiling, revealing a newly missing tooth.

"It's because they have the amusement park. People in Pyongyang don't do anything wrong because they're always happy," Chulho said with a scowl. "Isn't that right, fancy-pants Pyongyang boy?"

"What happened to your tooth?" I asked Young-bum, hoping to change the subject. I knew there was no way we would go to an execution. Joseon didn't kill people. The government just sent people who were bad to labor or political prison camps.

"Got in a fight. Lost it," he said matter-of-factly, drawing his tongue over the gap in his teeth. He seemed actually proud to have lost a tooth.

"Oh," I replied. I wanted to ask him more. Boys also don't fight unless it was in the *sojo,* and I knew from my father that there were no tae kwon do clubs in Gyeong-seong. Nothing these two boys said made sense.

"You still don't get it," Chulho said. "Life isn't good here. Ask your dad where he goes every day. Ask him what it's like in that factory of his."

"I'll do that," I snapped. What I really wanted to say to this guy was "Leave me alone."

I ARRIVED AT SCHOOL THE NEXT MORNING AND TOOK MY place at the front of the assembly. As school captain, my job was to ensure that the entire student body stood in straight lines and at attention, saluting the national flag of Joseon, followed by pledging allegiance that we would always be prepared to fight for our country. Beside me stood Young-bum, holding a pole with the school flag tied to the end. On our left arms, he and I wore bands indicating our school ranks. My band had three red lines and three stars because I was student president. His had three red lines and one star because he had a lower ranking.

As school captain, I was responsible for many things, including taking attendance. I walked down the lines of students, stiff-backed and knees bending high as if I were marching in a military parade, collecting the number of students from each class's leader, or *boon-dan-we-won-jang*. Then I returned to my place at the front of the assembly and called out: "All students' attention to the manager."

Then, to the *so-nyon-dan* manager, I said: "*So-nyon-dan*, two hundred students out of a total of three hundred are gathered in front of you."

"Stand at ease," the *so-nyon-dan* manager said to me.

"Stand at ease!" I hollered to the classes.

"Young-bum," I leaned toward him and whispered. "Where have all the students gone? This week we've lost another twenty."

"Hmm," he hummed, watching his flag droop. There was no wind. "I think they're trading their textbooks and clothes at markets in nearby towns or they've moved to another city so their parents can find food."

"Oh." I laughed out loud. I got it finally. "I guess these children and their families must have done something wrong against the government, like give military secrets to the South. That's why they've been abandoned and have no food. That's why some people up here have to eat squirrel. Thank you for clarifying," I said to Young-bum.

I turned my attention back to the students standing in front of me, smug in the knowledge that I'd finally figured out why Chulho and Young-bum say life is so terrible up here. It's because people outside Pyongyang *are bad.*

"Psst! Psst!" Young-bum hissed. I turned slowly and looked at him. "Do you really believe that?" he asked with real surprise in his voice.

"Yes," I replied with a nod, my tone of voice confident and assured.

"Today, students, we are going to an execution," the *so-nyon-dan* manager announced into a bullhorn with no emotion, almost casually, as if an execution were something the students went to regularly.

I jumped, both at the sudden noise of the bullhorn and at what was said.

Young-bum leaned over and whispered to me, "Today, your real-life education begins."

The *boon-dan-we-won-jang* called the classes to attention. When we set off on our march, I trailed behind the *so-nyon-dan* manager, and in order of age, from youngest to oldest, the rest of the school followed me. As we marched, the students sang songs about the great leader, Kim Il-sung, and Kim Jong-il. They sang loudly, sometimes shouting, so much so that my ears began to ring. Every now and then I could hear Sangchul's voice above the others. Surprising me, though, I could also hear Young-bum belting out the lyrics in a contralto octave, as if he were the *buk* in an off-tune symphony orchestra.

THE *SO-NYON-DAN* MANAGER HAD ME STOP ON THE BANK of the Gyeong-seong River, not far from the Ryongcheon railroad bridge. We joined hundreds of students from other schools as well as adults, many standing on tiptoe and facing what appeared to be two poles. A policeman had me lead my school to the front, where he instructed me to tell the others to sit on a dry patch of ground that was covered in pebbles and dust.

To the left was a white tent, on the front of which was Joseon's national emblem, which included pictures of Sup'ung Dam and Baekdu Mountain, a beam of light, and a five-pointed red star. The two long poles were in front of me. On the right was a table, on top of which were photographs framed in gold of Kim Il-sung and Kim Jong-il. When the sun's rays hit the picture frames, beams of light fanned out into the crowd, making me feel as if our eternal leaders were there with us, watching.

"Be a man!" Young-bum, still beside me, mumbled into my ear. "Don't look away. The first execution will be the hardest. After that, you'll get used to seeing death." He then laughed under his breath, a sinister cackle, as if he were the village idiot laughing at his own joke.

I remained stone-faced. I had no idea what was going on.

A gruff-looking police officer called us to attention by speaking into the bullhorn, introducing the judge, who walked to the center of the makeshift stage. The judge took the bullhorn from the police officer and called out a name.

My eyes moved to some fluttering behind the white tent. Two police officers finally emerged, each holding an arm of a middle-aged man whose hands were tied together by a piece of rough-looking rope. The man, who I guessed was the criminal, had skin the color of rock, and his legs were no bigger than a small child's. His body trembled as the policemen used more rope to tie him by his torso and legs to the pole. When the policemen stepped away, the man stared into the sky, and urine dripped down one of the legs of his pants and onto his bare feet.

The judge listed the man's crimes, the main one of which was that he had stolen copper and electrical wire from a local factory and was caught trying to cross the Duman River into China with the goods. The judge said the man had committed high treason, and for that, the prisoner was sentenced to death.

Bang, bang, bang.

Bang, bang, bang.

Bang, bang, bang.

The nine gunshots came from out of nowhere, fired by three police officers who I hadn't even noticed had taken positions close to me. Each of them shot the prisoner three times. The first pistol was aimed at the man's chest, the second at his abdomen or legs, the third at his head.

I jumped so high Young-bum reached over and held me down so I wouldn't do it again. I pinched my eyes tightly shut, but Young-bum said I needed to watch. "The police and the so-nyon-dan manager will think you're a traitor if you don't," he hissed.

I stared at this so-called criminal, his head hanging on his chest, his body crumpling under his weight, pools of blood bubbling up under his clothes and spreading out at his feet like a tide creeping in.

"See, even in death, the criminal has to bow down to the government," Young-bum whispered to me. "It's a lesson to us all: Don't commit crimes."

I looked at the three policemen who had shot him. They were reloading their pistols.

Next, police officers dragged a woman with shorn hair who looked about my mother's age toward the other pole. A dirty white cloth was dangling from her mouth, and her eyes were wild, darting back and forth, as if she were the tiger at the Pyongyang zoo. Someone in the crowd shouted, "Traitor!" and soon Chulho and Young-bum led a chorus of students chanting, "Traitor. Spy. We have to kill you! Kill you! All of you!"

The judge called into the bullhorn to get the crowd to quiet down. I wanted to cover my ears so I didn't have to hear these words or the bullets crack and whiz through the air again. I wanted to wake up and find myself back in Pyongyang, under my cotton sheets, knowing Bo-Cho was asleep in his doghouse—which wasn't much smaller than the house I lived in now. I wanted to return to my home city, with its palaces that glittered in the sunlight; its theaters, bronze monuments, skating rinks, hotels, and exhibition halls that rose up from the ground and lifted us all up, too—a city in the sky, that's what I thought of Pyongyang. Pyongyang, with its fountains, amusement park, forests . . . and silver escalators in the metro, polished every day by workers. In Pyongyang, everything about life was precise and known. And in Pyongyang, I had been taught that treason meant a person had sold Joseon secrets to the South or to the Americans, secrets that could put us all back to where we were under the Japanese: ruled by foreigners and oppressed. Treason meant the person and his or her family had to live in a labor or political prison camp. Our government didn't kill people . . .

". . . met a South Korean Christian missionary in China, who was helping her plan to escape to the South." The judge's words dug into me, his words about this woman slumping now in front of me, tied to the second stake, this woman with saliva frothing from her mouth, this woman wearing torn and dirty pants and a top that was just a darker shade of her dirty and malnourished skin. "Chinese police discovered her before she could leave and deported her to Joseon, where she stands before you . . ."

"Treason!" someone called out from the crowd.

This time, the sound of the guns' aftershock dug deep into my eardrums, causing a buzzing in my head. Sounds became muffled. I could see Young-bum's and Chulho's lips moving, but their voices sounded as if they were underwater.

I felt dizzy and sick.

CHAPTER

7

By the time I flung open the front door to my house, I was short of breath, still dizzy and nauseous, and feeling as though I was about to pass out. At least my hearing had come back. I knew this because I heard my classmates shouting goodbye and "Great execution" to one another as we went to our various homes for lunch.

I lay down on my mat, gasping for air.

"What happened?" my mother asked.

I jumped, despite her voice that cooed softly like a dove's.

"Shush, shush," she said, sitting down beside me and rubbing my forehead.

"Y-y-you're home early," I spluttered.

"What's the matter? You're upset about something?"

"I . . . at school . . . I . . . ," I began, but I wasn't clear. I was struggling to breathe, taking in big gulps of air. "We went . . . to . . . an execution . . . ," I somehow eventually managed to get out.

My mother moaned and knelt down beside me. "Your father and I wanted to protect you from that," she said, her voice heavy, as if a rain cloud had moved on top of her.

"Why didn't we see these things in Pyongyang?"

My mother shook her head.

"Why didn't you tell me people were being executed out in public like this, for crimes . . . that seem so . . ."

"Petty?" she asked. I nodded. "Your father and I wanted to protect you," she repeated.

"What else are you protecting me from?"

My mother shook her head again. "Nothing," she whispered, but I didn't believe her.

"Is it true what the boys at school say? Is Joseon starving? Are people doing things—wrong things—because they're desperate to eat?"

My mother's eyes filled with tears. She tried to look away, but I touched her face ever so lightly, enough to force her to look at me.

"Tell me the truth."

"Yes," my mother muttered.

"But we have food!" *Lots of food*, I thought.

"Only because we have won that your father has saved from Pyongyang." I could hear the knot in her throat as she talked. I could feel the knot in mine forming. I wanted to believe Chulho and Young-bum were the ones lying, not my parents.

I studied my mother's face: her eyes, which were lined in dark circles and creased in the corners with wrinkles she didn't have a few months earlier; her cheeks, which were sinking into her mouth, making her cheekbones look severe. She was no longer young or like that sunset. Something about her was changing.

"Your father didn't want you to know," she said slowly, covering her mouth and talking in a low voice. "He wanted you to feel safe. He's buying food at the markets with won he saved from his job in Pyongyang."

I heard heavy footsteps approaching the front door. "*Abeoji!*" I exclaimed. "*Eomeoni,* I need to know. Please tell me. We're not on vacation. Why did we leave Pyongyang?"

"Don't tell him we spoke," my mother whispered, ignoring my question. She jumped up, wiped her eyes, and smoothed down her black cotton top and slacks. "Men in Joseon are measured by their position and loyalty to the government," she said as she pulled me to my feet and brushed my hair with her fingers. "Your father is seen as a failure now. But he can bear all those bad looks and all the gossip . . . He can bear it all, except for one thing."

"What?" I whispered as we heard the door latch.

"The thought of you thinking of him as a failure, too," she whispered back.

¤ ¤ ¤

RY TIME I NEARED SLEEP, THE IMAGE OF ONE OF THE dead prisoners popped into my head. I'd hear the gunshots as if I were still on the execution field, and I'd sit bolt upright. All I could think about was what my father could have possibly done to lead to his fall from a very tall ladder. He didn't travel, at least not in the past few years, so there was no way he could have told our enemies military secrets. He went to work every weekday; he took part in all his required party activities. He loved and was devoted to Joseon.

"What did he do?" I found myself asking out loud.

The next day at school, I was so tired I wanted to slip under my desk and sleep. I pinched my legs hard to wake myself up. Young-bum noticed, leaned over, and asked me if I was all right. I waved him off. I didn't want him to know that I was confused and upset and that, well, maybe he and Chulho had been telling me the truth all along.

AS THE WEEKS WORE ON, I BEGAN TO SIT AND LISTEN TO Chulho, Young-bum, and their friends during our breaks, hearing about their struggles to find food. Chulho talked about how the forests were a great place to catch chipmunks. "There are so many," he said, "that no matter how many hungry people trample the ground up there, there are always more chipmunks."

"And they taste like chicken," Young-bum said, beaming.

I shuddered.

I was pretending to read my book when I overheard Young-bum tell some of the boys at school that his mother had died and that his father had left a few months earlier in search of food. He hadn't returned.

Every week when I took attendance as student council president, at least five more children had disappeared. Some I saw return a few days or weeks later. Most never showed up again, though.

One day, when the azaleas had begun to wilt and the begonias now colored the grasses, Chulho and I found ourselves alone together under a giant weeping willow on the school grounds. I put down my textbook about Kim Il-sung's childhood that I wasn't really reading anyway and asked him haphazardly if he knew where the students were going.

"Some of the girls are being married off to old Chinese men—some old enough to be their grandfathers," he replied in a tone of voice that made me feel as though I were the only one who didn't know this.

"Why?" I asked. I was finally going to take his bait. I was finally prepared to hear his stories. Believe them, though? That was something else.

"Families can get a lot of won for selling girls to Chinese men. The family might even get food sent back across the border if the husband is good."

Chulho then spat a huge gob of saliva as far as he could.

"And what about the boys?" I asked, spitting, too, trying to act cool.

"They become slave laborers on farms or in mines in China . . . farms and mines owned by Koreans—Koreans who have lived in China since before the Japanese army invaded the Korean Peninsula."

"Huh," I said, scratching my forehead. I was thinking to myself, *Shouldn't these Korean people in China be nicer to Koreans coming from here?*

"You do know that there are many Koreans in China, families and descendants of people who moved there during the Japanese era, right? Kim Il-sung started his guerrilla army in China, you know. Those Korean people the Chinese government considers citizens," Chulho pressed on, as if reading my mind and knowing what I was thinking. "But Koreans coming from Joseon . . . the Chinese view them as criminals. Chinese police hunt us down, beat us up, and then send us back to Joseon, where we're beaten again and sent to jails and . . ." His voice trailed off. He pursed his lips and shook his head slowly. "The Chinese hate us," he eventually continued. "We're like rats to them. They do everything they can to exterminate us if we step over onto their side of the border. In fact, everyone hates us—the West, the South, even Pyongyang. Those fat people in the capital would like to pretend everyone outside the city doesn't exist."

I didn't say anything. I didn't know what to say. I was book-smart. But the truth? If what Chulho said was half true, I knew nothing.

"Lots of people outside of Pyongyang are now trying to go to China to connect with family who have lived there since before liberation," Chulho continued, as if somehow he knew to just keep talking, to give me more information, that he was my new teacher. "Joseon people trade things, like dried pollack and squid from the coast, dried herbs, mushrooms, and metal. If they can sell enough, earn enough won in China, they can live a good life in North Korea, bribing police and border guards to let them go back and forth across the river. They can even start regular businesses. It's only the poor who are doomed in Joseon. The poor who can't afford to bribe officials. It's the poor we see executed. Never the rich."

Chulho and I sat for a long while in silence. At one point I closed my eyes and tilted my head up to catch the warm rays of the sun. As I did so, I listened to the calls of some thrush and starlings. I thought of *eomeoni* and *abeoji* and when they took me to the State Symphony Orchestra at the Grand Theater in Pyongyang. As I drifted further into my thoughts, I could even hear the violin concerto dedicated to our eternal father that played that night.

For a moment, just a brief moment, I forgot where I was and realized I didn't remember much of Pyongyang, except things like going to the symphony. In fact, I wondered if I'd ever lived there at all, even though I'd been here, in Gyeong-seong, for only a few months. But then I remembered something about Pyongyang, making it real again. One midsummer, when I was maybe six, my maternal grandfather, *hal-abeoji*, stayed with us. One afternoon, when the sky turned black and the air suddenly stopped moving, he said to me: "Have you not noticed that right before a storm, the leaves stop wrestling against the wind, the birds no longer sing their lullabies, and time stops moving forward?" Before I could answer, thunder groaned in the distance, and lightning flashed across the sky.

THE WISTFUL, HAZY DAYS OF SUMMER SOON FELL OVER Gyeong-seong. At first, I was too intoxicated by the heat and humidity and the country scents of leaves and fresh-cut grasses to notice that our meals had largely become cheap corn rice.

I realized for the first time that I was hungry when the August full moon hung low in the sky. I was on school holiday, not doing much of anything except listening to Chulho and Young-bum. My father had taken a break from work, too, and I went with him as he met with neighbors and hiked the forest paths.

An ache had formed in my stomach, a wanting, a yearning, a desire that could not be filled. As I'd lick my bowls dry of all broth, my insides were still crying out for more. For entire mornings, I'd sit under the willow tree in the school yard and watch the swallows skirting from tree branch to tree branch. Other times, though, I'd have so much energy I'd run up and down the mountains, getting exercise to replace the tae kwon do I was no longer doing. Every third or fourth day, Young-bum and I would slink off into the fields and lift rocks as weights, hoping to become like our classmate Min-gook, whose body was agile and strong.

One night just days before school was to start again, I made a bonfire outside our home. *Abeoji, eomeoni,* and I roasted some corn, fresh and still in its husk. Afterward, *abeoji* and I lingered behind, watching the embers turn blue.

"I'm only going to work two days a week to make sure I am there for self-criticism and to take part in party meetings," he said just as I was about to call it a night and head to bed. I stopped dead in my tracks and turned slowly. My father was still staring into the fire. But he must have known I was looking at him, for he pressed on.

"There are no rations. It's a waste of time for me to even show up."

I swallowed hard as I sat back down beside my father on a dead tree trunk we had pulled up together from the riverbank earlier in the day.

Eomeoni sat down beside me and told me next that she, too, was only going to work two days a week.

"What are we going to do?" I asked when they had both finished speaking. I suddenly remembered something else from Pyongyang. *Hal-abeoji* had also told me during that visit when I was about six that inside ourselves we already know the things that will happen to us in life. We spend our days just waiting for them to be revealed. I felt that now more than ever. I had been expecting this conversation.

"On the days we don't work, your mother and I are going to the forests to pick and hunt for food, like small animals and herbs, fungus and wild vegetables," *abeoji* continued. I thought of the squirrel Chulho was eating the day I met him. I felt a chill.

"I want to come with you," I said, surprising even myself.

I waited for my father's response. Nothing.

"There's no point in my going back to school," I continued. "I've already learned everything they teach there."

"You need to study," my mother finally cut in.

"No," I said quietly. "I need food, not knowledge." I was shaking now, for I had never defied my parents before.

My mother began to sob, and my father breathed heavily. I started to tremble. But I wasn't going to back down. "*Eomeoni. Abeoji*," I began, this time slowly and trying to remain calm. "The boys at school—they come and go. They earn won with their families. They catch their own squirrels, mice, and, well, anything, *anything*, that they can eat. Take me with you. I want to help us find food."

THE NEXT DAY, I HEADED TO THE MARKET WITH MY KOREAN language and geometry textbooks under my arm. My plan was to trade the books for tofu, cabbage, and corn oil.

As I crossed the Ha-myeon Bridge onto the gravel road that led into the market, I saw Chulho sitting off to the side. As I neared, he looked up at me with bloodshot eyes, his face lined in dark shadows and peppered with stubble.

"I've never asked," I said, stopping in front of him. "Do you sleep outside?"

"Yeah, sometimes," he said, rubbing his head. "My mom and dad—well, same story as everyone else. They left to find food . . . didn't come back. What are you doing, Pyongyang fancy-pants?" He pointed to my books.

"Selling these," I said, sitting down beside him. We faced the road, looking out at the merchants heading into the market to sell their goods.

"So the fancy-pants Pyongyang family has finally fallen on hard times," he said dryly.

I shrugged. "I guess so." No point escaping the truth anymore. "Chulho, my friend," I said, wrapping an arm around him. "We've been on hard times since we left that fancy-pants city."

We both laughed.

"Why did you leave Pyongyang?" he asked next. "I mean, the entire town has their ideas, but none of us knows for sure."

"I don't know," I said with another shrug. I really didn't know.

"Someone will use the pages of those books for toilet paper or fire kindling or women will plug up their monthly cycles," Chulho explained, pointing to my books again.

"Imagine that," I said, holding up my Korean language book. "Our mamas can study while they go to the washroom."

"School is a luxury for the kids who are fat," Chulho added.

Just then I spied Min-gook trudging up the road like a tank. He was whistling "We Are Kid Scouts," the song from the cartoon *Squirrel and Hedgehog*. I shook my head. "No matter how much Young-bum and I try, we will never be in shape like this guy," I said with a groan as Min-gook spied us, waved, and started heading our way. "How does he keep so fit?"

Chulho grunted. "He used to make money as a pull-cart operator. He also carried his mother, who just died from a hunger disease. For more than a year, his mom couldn't walk, and he would carry her everywhere."

Min-gook sat down and pulled out from underneath his shirt a twisted bread stick. My mouth began to water.

"Where did you get that?" I asked. He broke the bread into three pieces and handed one to me. I popped it into my mouth and sucked on it, letting it dissolve slowly. I hadn't tasted anything so good in a long time.

"At the market," Min-gook replied with a wide smile. "I sold some of my mother's pots and pans. After I bought corn rice and eggs, as well as some alcohol for my father, I, well . . . I got me some dessert." He ate his piece more slowly, dotting the front of his shirt with bread crumbs.

Chulho turned away from the road and lit up a smoke.

"Don't," I said, swatting the cigarette away from his hand. "You'll get into trouble for being a kid smoking in public."

"Trust me," he said, rolling his eyes and picking up the cigarette. "The party leaders in Gyeong-seong have way more to worry about than me smoking in a public place."

"But what will people think?" I asked, truly aghast. I mean, what could come next up here?

"Trust me," Chulho repeated, using the same sarcastic tone. "People have a lot more to worry about than me smoking in a public place. Nobody, fancy-pants Pyongyang boy, cares! Now leave me to smoke alone in peace."

I sighed and turned back to Min-gook. "How did you sell your things? I mean, do you just walk into the market and hold the items up, waiting for someone to approach you?"

"No," Min-gook replied. "You go up to people and ask them if they want to buy what you're selling. But be careful not to hold what you're selling too loose. Someone will grab them from you. Lots of thieves in the market. What are you selling?" he then asked.

I held up the books. He hummed. "I sold mine last winter. The school doesn't seem to care that students don't hand the books back anymore at the end of the school year. Everyone kind of knows where they're going. I didn't buy the bun," he then added, as if I had asked. "I lifted it from the woman who'd sold me the eggs."

I gasped. "Aren't you afraid of stealing? I mean, you could go to prison," I said.

Min-gook and Chulho looked at each other and then sighed.

"People expect stealing now," Chulho said in that voice again, as if I were a small child and not very bright. "Sure, if we're caught, we could be in trouble. But . . . well . . . what else are we supposed to do?"

Too many thoughts were swimming around in my head: kids smoking, kids stealing . . .

"I've quit school," I said, feeling I had to change the subject or else I'd end up with one major headache.

"We all knew it was just a matter of time," Chulho said, patting me on the back, as if welcoming me to his club. "I have, too. May as well enjoy what time we have left on this planet. Walk on the wild side before you die."

"We're not going to die," I scoffed. But as I said this, I had that sinking feeling again that I already knew this wasn't true.

Chulho chuckled. "You think so? I buried my younger brother a week ago," he said with no emotion, no sadness, no regrets. It just was.

"Why didn't you tell me—us—your classmates?" I exclaimed. "I would have come by and paid my respects."

"Are you joking?" Chulho said, blowing rings of smoke into the air. This time he wasn't laughing.

"No. I'm not," I said in a low voice.

"Every day we're burying kids at the foot of the mountain," Chulho said. "Soon there won't be any space left in the ground. My brother was just one ceremony of about forty you've missed."

THAT EVENING, AFTER I SOLD MY TEXTBOOKS, *ABEOJI* AND I made backpacks by sewing together old pairs of pants.

On the days *abeoji* didn't go into work, we'd head out at dawn, with the mist still covering the fields, and collect arrowroot, dandelions, and pine and elm tree bark, which my mother would make into broth for our soup or sell at the market. My father and I cut down small trees for firewood that we piled inside the house, because a neighbor had warned *abeoji* that thieves were taking anything that was left outside at night. Soon there was so much wood in the house there was little room for us to walk around.

In the forests, *abeoji* and I caught chipmunks by pouring water from the river into their holes. The little creatures would scamper out to avoid being drowned. As they did, we would strike their heads and torsos with our knives. When they were dead, we'd skin them, cut off the meat, skewer some of the flesh onto sticks, and roast it over the fire. My mother would smoke the rest and then store the meat in an underground cupboard my father and I dug.

The first time I saw a snake, I jumped into some ferns, screaming so loudly I scared a couple of magpies, which squawked at me before flying away. My father was stone-faced and shaking his head, waving for me to come back. He pointed at the brown snake that had tiny yellow and green flecks, then to a rock about the size of my head. He motioned for me to throw it.

I held the rock up high over my head, the way Young-bum and I had been lifting weights. I then crept up behind the snake, which was nearing a decaying log that was covered in moss and armies of ants. If the snake got inside the log, I would never be able to catch it. I closed my eyes and threw the rock as hard as I could.

Thump.

My father had to pry open my eyelids to make me look. The rock had nearly split the snake in two. I had killed it.

My father and I decided to stay in the forest for the night so that we could get a jump start in the morning collecting wild vegetables and *deodeok* root. For our bed, we laid a sheet of plastic on top of some dead leaves in a clearing. For dinner, we roasted the snake meat on skewers over the fire. Afterward, we both tried to sleep but couldn't. My father moved in close beside me and wrapped his arms around me. I rolled onto my back, and the two of us looked up at the stars. "On an island called Jeju, people feared snakes," he started to tell me. "They would never kill them, for they are seen as symbols of wealth."

"*Abeoji,* don't tell me that now, when all the snake has been eaten," I scolded. I already felt bad enough for having killed it. I didn't want to see its death as a sign that I'd be poor for the rest of my life.

"There is more," he continued. "It's believed that if you cut off the tail of a snake that's still alive, it will come to kill you at night when you're sleeping, seeking revenge."

I shivered. "I don't like these stories, *abeoji*. Tell me a happy story."

"Okay, how is this, then? In Jeju, they believe in a goddess named Chilseong, who by some accounts had seven daughters. Others say she had seven sons. Some believe Chilseong came from China, cast ashore in a metal box. Others say she was a star who wanted to experience being human, so she and her children, also stars, were born as snakes. One thing both sides believe is that when their human lives came to an end, Chilseong and her children returned to the sky. They're the seven stars of the Ursa Major, or the Big Dipper. Chilseong is considered the brightest star in the constellation. Look," he said, pointing. "Chilseong and her children shine the brightest of all the stars and are thought to protect the Korean people from misfortune and pain. Chilseong, being a mother, watches over children. Whenever you feel lost or in pain, *adeul*, find Chilseong and call out for her help."

"*Abeoji*," I said after a while. "What do people believe in Joseon?"

"Well," he started slowly, "I've heard that some people, especially in the villages, believe in spirits, the *shan-shin-ryong-nim*, which live in caves. These are good spirits, not spirits of unhappy people looking to hurt the living."

"Like the *yu-ryeong*," I cut in.

"Yeah, like the *yu-ryeong*—ghosts who are cursed. People take clear water in big jugs and food and lay it before these caves where they believe the *shan-shin-ryong-nim* live. It's an offering, to ask the *shan-shin-ryong-nim* for things such as food and maybe better jobs, a good marriage for their son or daughter or good school results for their smaller children."

I thought hard about *abejoi*'s words. It struck me as odd that starving people would offer up food to the *shan-shin-ryong-nim*. "*Abeoji*, what do people believe in Pyongyang?"

"In Kim Il-sung and now the general, Kim Jong-il," he replied a little too stiffly, as though he were annoyed.

"That's all?" I continued.

"Pretty much," he said.

I wanted to touch his face then, have him look at me, and tell me what he did that forced us to leave Pyongyang. I wanted to know what he believed in. But I heard him sigh. I could tell he felt defeated now, and I decided against the idea. Instead, I slipped my left hand into his and laid my head on his shoulder.

8

The winter of 1998 was hard. My mother stored dried vegetables as well as radishes and potatoes in our underground cupboard in the backyard. On top of that, I had used evergreen boughs to hide the location of the freezer from thieves. But while no thieves found our stash, our stored food had to be rationed nonetheless.

I was hungry every day.

I was also bored.

When the animals hibernated and the ground was frozen, I'd wake before my mother and father, shimmy to the window, and peer out at the snow. I'd long since sold my sketchbook at the market. Now my only canvas was the thin layer of ice on the inside of the windowpane. Using a fingernail, I'd sketch pictures of the 105 army tank and combat airplanes. I'd do this for a while and then slump back down onto my mat, light-headed, with my feet and hands pricked by pins and needles. *Eomeoni* said these were symptoms of malnutrition.

By the end of January our supply of squirrel, chipmunk, rabbit, and snake had all gone. We had one meal a day of corn rice and some cabbage or pickled radish.

I wasn't the only one suffering from hunger. The neighbor men would visit our home sometimes with bottles of alcohol, *sool*, that they would drink with my father. It took only a glass for the men to begin slurring their words. "Drunk" was the word *eomeoni* used to describe them as she shooed me into the other room away from them. But I would press my ear up to the wall and listen to them. As the men got drunk, they would hound my father for information from Pyongyang, including what General Kim Jong-il was going to do next about this thing called a famine.

My father would answer their questions as if he were one of the government representatives who delivered information to us on Joseon's Central TV station back in Pyongyang: formal and evasive. He always skirted around the men's questions and toed the party line, which in the case of this famine thing was that Joseon's enemies were responsible and that all of us had to be strong and consider what we were going through as an Arduous Walk, like what Kim Il-sung did when he ousted the Japanese.

Over time, the neighbor men shrunk before my eyes until two of them were no bigger than their own sons, who were just a little older than me. The skin on the men's faces sagged, making them appear years older than I knew they actually were. As they withered away, their eyes remained the same size and began to stick out like saucers. Looking at them made me think of the *yu-ryeong*—legless, floating ghosts that people left on earth after they died because they hadn't completed some mission, like protecting a family member or seeking revenge on someone else.

At least now I knew why the principal and teacher swam in their suits. Now I, too, had to use a rope to tie my pants around my waist to keep them from falling down. So did Young-bum. The few times we got together, he and I would look out my window at the smaller children, many now bowlegged like frogs. We called out to them: *"Gae-gu-ri."*

Eomeoni would slap us across the back of the heads and tell us not to be so rude.

"They're sick," she'd admonish. "They're suffering from rickets. They need the oil from pollack fish to help them get better." Her own hair was dry and splitting, her fingernails cracking. Before my eyes, she was wasting away, too. But then she'd sing in a soft voice *"Dondolari"* or *"Shagwa-poongnyon,"* a bumper year of apples, and I'd be reminded all over again of the time I saw her do the fan dance.

IN MARCH 1998, A WEEK BEFORE MY ELEVENTH BIRTHDAY, at night as we kept warm by the wood fire before bedtime, my father announced that he was going to China.

As he spoke, images flashed across my mind of executed prisoners wilting on the posts after having been shot nine times. Images of the blood, of their frantic eyes . . . "No!" I finally screamed, cutting him off midsentence as he explained how he was getting in and out of China. "You can't go. You'll be killed."

Both *eomeoni* and *abeoji* crawled up beside me. They stroked my back and told me everything would be all right. "Lots of people are going to China," *eomeoni* explained. "The border guards can be bribed."

"The neighbors and I have a plan," *abeoji* cut in.

I pulled myself into a tight ball and covered my ears with my hands. I started to rock back and forth on my haunches, humming to myself. I didn't want to hear. But I did.

"The neighbors and I are going to pay the guards to let us cross over the river at the lowest point, where it's still frozen. One of the neighbors has done it before. We're going to pay the same guards to let us come back a week later, just before spring thaw. It's safe."

I rolled onto my back and looked up at him. "What are you going to do in China? Steal? Work for a Korean on his farm as a slave?"

"No," he said with a laugh.

"I have my medals," he went on, his voice lower. "While I don't want to sell them, they're made of precious metals. They should fetch enough won for me to start a business buying white rice, sugar, and oil, which I'll bring back with me and sell here. I'm going to start trading goods back and forth."

"You agree to this?" I asked, looking to *eomeoni*.

She nodded.

"But it's illegal!"

"I also want to get you something special for your birthday . . . a cake . . . a candy . . . ," he said, ignoring my statement. "No—a rice cake?"

"We'll get through this," my mother added, leaning over and kissing my cheek. "*Abeoji* will be back in one week, promise."

"One week!" my father said. "Just one week."

WHEN ABEOJI *WALKED THROUGH THE DOOR, A WAVE OF fresh, pine-scented air came, too, swirling around the room the way Sangchul's voice did at the train station. His face was rosy, wind-touched, and his eyes sparkled as if he were a young man again.*

He lugged a large blue duffel bag. Like a child unwrapping a birthday present, eomeoni *began pulling items out of the bag: white rice, a block of tofu, some dried fish, cabbage, peppers, sugar, oils . . . While she did this,* abeoji *reached under his coat and handed me a paper bag. "Happy birthday," he whispered, ruffling my hair.*

He didn't need to tell me what was in the bag. I knew. Rice cakes, sweetened and with sesame sprinkles, and a serving of mashed red beans.

As I ate, my eyes moved up and down abeoji. *He wore a new pair of black wool pants and a warm gray sweater underneath a new navy-blue wool coat with big gold buttons.* Eomeoni *held up a dress in soft yellow, like the color of a canary; it was a dress she would have worn to the military parade on the Day of the Sun.*

I woke then and patted down my bedding, hoping that it wasn't a dream and that *abeoji* was lying beside me. Then I saw it, the ice inside the windowpane, the dull walls, and my mother's bedding, blankets of which were scattered across the floor. *Abeoji* was not home.

I crept out of bed and crawled to the wall where I had tacked a piece of paper. On the paper I had drawn squares, each of which represented a day of the week. I took my pencil, now a stub, and put an X through Monday. This was the fourth day *abeoji* was gone. He had left on Friday.

I turned around, my stomach aching for food, and saw my mother sitting on her knees in the other room, her back facing me. She was mumbling words I couldn't quite make out. I felt, despite her nearness, that she was very far away.

"*Eomeoni*," I said softly, trying to get her attention.

I moved toward her on tiptoe until I was standing at her side. Her eyes were closed. Her features seemed softer, and her eyelashes glistened in the sun shining through the window. She looked as if she had been kissed by a cloud.

A weak smile crossed her face.

"What are you doing?" I asked, sitting down beside her.

"I'm praying," she said with her eyes still closed. "But shush." She put her finger to her lips. "You can't tell anyone."

"What does *praying* mean?"

Eomeoni took my hands into hers. For the first time since we left Pyongyang, she felt warm. "Some people talk to a higher power, a universal power, an energy, where our ancestors go to live after they die," she said. "That higher power listens and answers what we ask of it. We speak to that power in the form of prayers."

"Like asking Chilseong or *shan-shin-ryong-nim* to watch over us?"

"How do you know about these things?" she said, opening one eye and looking at me.

"*Abeoji*," I answered. "What do you pray for?" Whatever this prayer thing was, it made her look as she did when we lived in Pyongyang: like a butterfly.

"I pray for *abeoji* to be safe and to come home quickly," she said, closing her eyes again.

"I dreamed he came home," I whispered, "with rice cakes and nice clothes and . . ." My voice trailed off. A knot had formed in my throat. I didn't want to share my hopes and dreams, even with my mother. It seemed to me that as soon as I told anyone what I wanted, it was taken from me.

"What is that?" I asked her, pointing to a bowl by the wall in which she had placed fresh water.

My mother opened both her eyes this time. "Water is pure, and in offering it up to the power, we are showing it that we give to it, surrender, our most pure souls. The water represents us."

"Oh," I exclaimed, dipping a finger into the water. "If we're so clean, though, how come we get so dirty?"

My mother started to giggle then, the first time she'd laughed in months.

MY MOTHER AND I DID NOT SPEAK OF WHAT COULD HAVE happened to *abeoji*. We sat in silence at night, alone while together, listening to each other's breathing. *Abeoji's* absence lay like a heavy wool blanket between us that neither of us could lift. I looked to *eomeoni's* hope as a light leading me down a dark tunnel.

"Trust" was all she would whisper, as if in our silence I was speaking my worries to her. "Trust" was her answer, always, but I wasn't quite sure whom I was supposed to trust.

One morning after I awoke screaming from a nightmare in which I saw a strange white creature, half man, half monster, with fire for wings, I asked my mother to teach me how to pray.

She placed my hands together and raised them until they were the level of my chest. "Close your eyes and then talk in your head to that universal power. Tell it your fears and ask for guidance.

Chilseong and shan-shin-ryong-nim . . . , I began. Abeoji *is lost. Can you bring him home?* Eomeoni *and I need him. I miss him. I . . .*

I stopped on the word I wanted to say next. It just hurt too much to think it. But somehow my mother knew and finished the sentence for me. "I love him, too."

As the days wore on, I repeated my prayer to Chilseong and *shan-shin-ryong-nim* over and over again, slowly and then more quickly, silently, methodically, much as I once did in school with the sayings of our eternal leader, Kim Il-sung.

ON THE LONGEST DAY OF THE YEAR, AS MOSQUITOES AND blackflies attacked me while I picked berries near the Gyeong-seong River with *eomeoni*, she said that she was going to visit her sister, Nampo, in Wonsan. "There is nothing left to sell," she said in a low voice, sitting down on a large flat rock and dipping her toe into the water. I sat on the rock beside her. The frogs croaked around us.

"For how long?" I asked as a woodpecker knocked at a nearby tree.

"A week. Nampo's husband is in the navy. She will have food."

"When do we leave?"

"I want you to stay here," she said after a long pause. Her voice was drawn and tired.

I shook my head. "No," I said. "You're not leaving me."

"I'll be gone only a few days." She was fighting back tears. I could tell.

"What are you not saying to me?" I demanded so harshly I regretted asking the question as soon as I spoke it.

Eomeoni began to shake. I reached out and pulled her into my arms.

"Nothing," she said as I rocked her back and forth. "I'm keeping nothing from you. We need food, and Aunt will have it. I will be gone just a couple of days."

"Like *abeoji*," I spat out. I was hot and angry again. I wanted to punch something, anything I could find, except *eomeoni*. I couldn't let her leave me. I gripped the bottom of her shirt. "I'm coming with you no matter what," I cried out as tears started to fall.

It took a while to convince her I had to go with her. She kept shaking her head and saying, "No. It's too dangerous to come with me." But she wouldn't tell me what those dangers were, so I pressed and pressed on, determined not to be left alone.

Finally, she nodded and whispered yes.

I stayed awake well into the night, listening to the crickets strumming their lullabies and the occasional hooting of an owl. I refused to close my eyes. Even when my mother went to the outhouse, I followed. I wanted to make sure she didn't leave without me.

I felt guilty. I was a bad son. But the truth was, I didn't trust her.

*deul*," I heard my mother say as I slipped in and out of waking and dreaming.

Then I remembered the day before: my mother's plan to go to Nampo for food.

I remembered my vow not to fall asleep.

But I had.

My eyes popped open, and I sat bolt upright. My heart raced. I was perspiring, and my hands were clammy with nervousness. Light streamed in through the window, illuminating the dust and casting a long shadow across the floor. It was about midday.

I'd slept all morning.

I patted the bedding beside me where my mother's mat was still laid out. It was warm, as if she had just gotten up.

But she wasn't in the other room praying in front of her bowl.

I leaped up and ran outside.

"*Eomeoni!*" I shouted, heading first to the outhouse and throwing open the wooden door.

Not a sound. Not even the scampering feet of mice.

Barefooted, I walked around our tiny house and then down the dirt road. As my pace quickened, stones dug into the soft flesh of my soles. But I didn't care. I searched the train station, peering into the haggard faces of people waiting for trains. Frantically, zigzagging, I crossed the Ha-myeon Bridge and searched the market. I walked up to several women, thinking that from the back they were my mother. But when I tugged on their sleeves and they spun around, they were someone else's mother.

I then headed home, hoping that my mother had just gone to the fields to catch grasshoppers we could roast.

I pushed open the front door.

Inside was vacant.

Cold.

As the sky slid into twilight, I limped back to the road and collapsed on a small mound of earth off to the side. I then began to sob . . . I had lost Bo-Cho, my dreams of becoming a general, my schooling, Pyongyang, my piano, my doghouse, my father . . . my mother. I didn't stop crying until the day songs of the cicadas faded and the cooler melodies of the night insects took over. That's when I crawled back into the house, pushing open the front door with the palm of my hand and dragging myself to *eomeoni*'s bedding, where I wrapped myself in her scent.

¤ ¤ ¤

WHEN I AWOKE, IT WAS LIGHT AGAIN.

I didn't want to move, but then a flash moved through me, a hope that my mother was there, doing her prayers.

"*Eomeoni, Eomeoni . . .*" My voice echoed against the bare walls. Then I saw it, a letter, poking out from underneath her prayer bowl.

Son, it started, *there's some porridge in the pot. Have it when you are hungry.*

I pulled off the lid of our last remaining pot and, using my hands, began shoveling into my mouth the porridge made from ground vegetables and cornstarch. After I had finished and burped, I looked at the letter again.

Eomeoni had written more.

> *I'm going to Aunt's house to get food, and I will return home in seven days. You must stay at home. If there's no food, you must eat salt and drink water.*
>   *Mom*

I skulked outside and drew enough water from the well to fill the empty pot. Then I put it and the small box of salt beside my mat. I lay back down and stared up at a daddy longlegs crawling on the ceiling. "For a week, I will not move—to save energy," I told the creature, which paid me no attention.

I then closed my eyes and imagined eating pork and tofu fried with seaweed and the fried fish that *eomeoni* would make when she returned from Wonsan. I then thought of *abeoji* arriving home at the same time with bags full of new clothes and rice cakes. I would go back to school. Whatever *abeoji* had done, he would be forgiven, and we'd go back to Pyongyang, where I would return to the tae kwon do *sojo*. For the first time in a very long time, I dreamed of being a general, leading my unit in the Day of the Sun military parade.

ON THE MORNING OF THE SEVENTH DAY, I AWOKE SWIM-ming in perspiration. I pushed off my covers and, desperate for some water, tried to open my eyes to find the pot. But my eyelids were glued shut. I patted my face and discovered that my cheeks and eyelids had swelled up like a puffer fish. I sat up quickly and screamed.

"I'm blind. Help. *Help!*" But of course no one came. No one could hear me, or if they could, as Chulho would say, "They have enough problems of their own."

I crept toward where I hoped was *eomeoni*'s wedding chest. For a few seconds I fumbled with the lock, which I couldn't see because my eyes were still glued shut. Finally, I got the chest open and felt inside. There was nothing left of the sheets, towels, and gowns—even my father's army uniform that we had brought with us from Pyongyang was gone. We'd sold almost everything.

But the broken mirror I was looking for was there, on the bottom.

I took it out and lifted it toward where I thought my face would be.

I then used my fingers to jimmy open my eyes.

At first I saw shadows, and then streaks of light, and finally my reflection. Although I wasn't blind, what stared back at me wasn't good.

This time my scream was so shrill I scratched my vocal cords.

I was round and shiny like the balloons released on parade days. My face looked as if it were coated in candle wax. I realized with a jolt that the salt I had eaten for a week had made me retain so much water that I had become a beached whale. "I'm sick," I moaned. "I can't stay here like *eomeoni* asked me to do."

I pulled myself up by digging my fingernails into the wall. My legs were wobbly, and blood rushed to my head. I was going to faint. "You can't," I admonished myself.

I knew I stank of my own waste as I finally made it out the front door and headed down the road. I knew I looked like something dug up dead from the river. I knew I scared the children, as their mothers draped them in their arms and hastened them into their houses. But I knew I would die if I didn't press on.

My legs ached. I had chest pains, and my throat burned. An out-of-tune orchestra played in my head, *bang, clonk, dunk,* with the cymbal player as the soloist. Many times I stumbled and nearly fell, but something lifted me up, maybe those universal forces to whom I now prayed, and pushed me onward. Finally, I made it to Young-bum's door, newly painted a light blue, like the sky the day after a summer storm. Before I pushed it open, I thought: *How odd this country is. We're all starving, but the government still forces people to paint their houses.*

"What are you doing here?" Young-bum asked, his voice faltering when I fell into his house like a bouncing ball that didn't stop until it hit the far wall.

"Help me," I croaked as saliva dripped from the corners of my mouth. "I've had nothing to eat for a week but salt. I am carrying too much water."

Young-bum's lips trembled, and he eyed me suspiciously. "Who are you?" he asked, grabbing the shovel he and I used to dig up herbs. His hands trembled as he waved it in front of my face.

"It's me," I tried to call out, but I had little voice left from all my screaming. "It's me," I repeated. "We lift stones together as weights . . ."

"What happened to you?" Young-bum gasped, lowering the shovel.

I grunted. I moaned.

I tried to tell him that my mother had left and that I had nothing to eat. But before I could, I fell into his arms and passed out.

YOUNG-BUM HELD A CUP OF COOL WELL WATER TO MY LIPS. I took a few sips, spilling more on my shirt than I managed to swallow. He then placed in my hand a soft-boiled potato. "I stole it from the storage box next door," he explained. "I've got a pile."

I sat in the corner and tried sucking on the potato, because, in addition to everything else, my gums hurt and my throat was so damaged that swallowing felt like nails scratching a blackboard. I looked around Young-bum's house. I'd never been inside it before. The main room was smaller than mine, and it was just as sparse because most of his family's furniture, dishes, and clothes had been sold, too. My eyes landed on a lump on the ground beside the cooking fire. It was shaped like a small person. But it wasn't moving. I dug my heels into the ground and pushed my oversize body as far away from it as I could, until my back was flush up against the wall.

"It's my grandmother," Young-bum said, sitting down beside me. "She's sick. She's not dead," he assured me. "She has tuberculosis. She . . ." His voice trailed off. I stretched my swollen neck to look at him. He was crying. "She doesn't sleep much. She has night sweats and coughs. But when she does sleep, she is so peaceful, and I don't want to wake her," he said.

I forced myself to eat the potato, knowing it was the only way I could get rid of my swelling, and then drank more water.

When I was done, Young-bum grumbled something about going out for a while and that I should rest.

PROPPED UP AGAINST THE WALL, I LISTENED TO TWO women outside bickering over tofu. I could make out that one of the women had tried to sell it, but a *kotjebi*—a word I had never heard before—had stolen it. The way the women went on, I imagined this *kotjebi* to be some kind of wild, rabid dog with foam frothing from its mouth. "Kind of like what I must look like right now," I said to myself. I then started chuckling. But it hurt to laugh, so I stopped. I heard crying followed by scuffling and then slapping sounds. The two women were fighting.

I pulled myself up and looked around. Young-bum had placed his old school uniform beside me. As I reached to touch it, Young-bum came crashing in through the front door, breathing heavily, carrying a black bag made from an old shirt. He slammed the front door shut and slid to the floor. "*Shush*," he whispered to me.

The sound of running feet drew near. Then men's voices calling out to each other: "He's gone down this way!"

"No, this way!"

"What did you do?" I mouthed to Young-bum, who flicked his hand at me, which I interpreted as meaning that this wasn't a great time to ask.

After the voices and footsteps disappeared, Young-bum crawled to his grandmother's side and gently shook her shoulders. She moaned, then coughed up blood that splattered down her chin. Young-bum wiped it away with a towel. As he propped her head up on a pillow, she whimpered like a small child. Young-bum pulled some bottles from his black bag, clanking them together as he set them on the ground. He then poured some pills from one of the bottles and counted five in the palm of his hand.

Young-bum drew a cup of water from a pail and put it to his grandmother's lips so she could swallow the pills.

I could hear liquid swimming around in her lungs as she breathed. When Young-bum set her gently back down on her mat, she coughed up more blood into a cloth. The room filled with the stench of her illness, sweet and sour at the same time.

Young-bum made some porridge by grinding together corn, rice, soybean paste, and a watery, almost rotten, cucumber. He spoon-fed his grandmother, as if she were the child and not he.

After Young-bum had washed her down with another cloth, he told her what his day at school was like.

"I'm so far ahead in math that teacher said I should enter a math contest," he told her. All the while I was thinking that his school uniform was at the bottom of my mat and it seemed to me that he had spent the day in the market stealing instead.

"Teacher says if I keep up the good work, next year I might even become school captain . . ."

I didn't want to hear anymore. I pulled myself up, which was hard because I was still so bloated it was like heaving a large boulder over my head to get myself even to a standing position. I then headed outside to the outhouse.

When I finally plopped myself down on the toilet seat, I sat and listened to the bugs scampering around me, the twigs falling on the roof, and the wind stirring the long grasses in the nearby field. Eventually I just dozed off.

I AWOKE THE NEXT MORNING TO YOUNG-BUM'S PUNCHING my shoulder. "Get up," he said loudly, hurting my eardrums.

"What is it?" I asked, clamoring to sit up straight, which was now even harder since my body was cramped in addition to being swollen from sleeping in the outhouse all night. "Is Joseon being invaded?"

"Don't be stupid," he hissed, pulling me up. "No one is trying to invade us. Look, I can't tell my grandmother I'm not at school," Young-bum explained. "It would kill her to know I've quit. Come with me," he said.

I groaned. While I could tell the potassium in the potato had helped rid my body of some of its excess water, I was still pretty sick. My clothes were too tight, for one. I had torn the seam in the back of my pants, and two buttons had popped on my shirt. "I don't feel well," I moaned.

Young-bum helped me walk inside the house. "Here, put this on," he said, passing me his school uniform.

"I'm not going to school," I protested. "I quit last fall. I thought you had, too." I was whispering just in case his grandmother was awake and could hear.

"You're not going to school," he replied. "But your clothes are ripped. Wear my uniform. It was from before we had food problems . . . Before, when I was fat." He then began to tug off my pants.

I was too tired to even make a joke about his former weight or to protest his undressing me.

"Where are we going?" I asked instead as he zipped up the fly of my new pants. The length was okay, but they were tight.

"To your new kitchen," Young-bum answered, slipping a pair of his sneakers onto my feet. He tried to do up the laces but couldn't. I strained to look over my protruding stomach to see my feet, which seemed bigger than my head.

"Here, wear my father's old shoes," Young-bum said, handing me a pair of brown running shoes with holes in the soles. Before I could ask if there were any other shoes, Young-bum was heading out the front door.

For a while, we walked the road in silence, Young-bum having to slow his pace to match mine, which was not much faster than a turtle's crawl.

"Why were those men chasing you?" I finally asked, more just trying to fill the air between us with conversation than wanting an answer. I kind of guessed already he had stolen those pills for his grandmother.

"I couldn't afford grandmother's medicine yesterday," Young-bum said. "So I took it from the market."

"You mean you stole it," I said.

He grunted.

"What happened to your parents?" I asked next. He had never told me directly.

"My aunt took my mother away in an oxcart. My aunt said she was taking my mother to the doctor to fix her tuberculosis," he said, his voice distant, as if he were straining to remember something he had forgotten or maybe wanted to forget. "But we couldn't afford the medicine, and back then, I wasn't stealing, so she died before she got there . . . Well, we all died a bit then, I guess."

"I'm sorry," I whispered, and I really was.

"My father left to find food, said he was going to China, and he hasn't come back yet," he added.

"My mother went to Aunt's house to get food, too," I said after another long silence. "She told me she would be gone a week and to eat salt and drink water until she got back. That was, I think, about ten days ago." I wasn't keeping track this time. I guess, after my father, I was scared to.

Young-bum mumbled that he was sorry, too. I believed him.

"Are you taking me to the hospital?" I then quipped. "Is the hospital my new kitchen?"

Young-bum laughed. "What would be the point? The hospital doesn't have any medicines anymore, either. You have to buy what you need or steal it, and then take it to the doctor, who will make you pay him to tell you how much to take. It's just a waste of time. You get sick here, you fend for yourself—not like in Pyongyang, where I'm pretty sure they make sure their future generals never get sick. I bet your hospitals in Pyongyang are made out of silver, just like your metro's escalators."

I laughed then, too, not because what he said was funny, but because it was sort of true, except that our escalators weren't made out of silver. "My maternal grandfather is a doctor," I said in a weak voice. "Maybe," I added after a short pause, "you can help me find a way back to Pyongyang to find him."

Young-bum stopped suddenly and turned to face me. "You're joking, right?" he asked, studying my eyes.

I shrugged. "Yeah, maybe, kind of. No."

"Chulho and I believed you were just acting dumb when we told you about things going on in Joseon. But really . . . you don't know! Your family was *kicked out* of Pyongyang, fancy-pants," he said, "because Pyongyang people don't come here to live unless the government has told them to get out. And when Pyongyang fancy-pants people are asked to leave, they're stripped of everything. Everyone knew about your family the moment you arrived in that train station, all polished like those shiny metal escalators in the metro in the capital. Everyone talked behind your father's back about how a great star of the regime must have done something really bad to have fallen into a garbage heap like this."

I felt the knot in my throat grow tight. My father hadn't wanted me to know these things. I felt I was betraying him just by listening. But Young-bum was right. I had known everything he said all along, from the moment the light flickered and then went out and I saw the dead bird of prey on my way home from the tae kwon do *sojo*.

"You can't go back to Pyongyang," Young-bum continued, his voice light and soft as if he genuinely wanted to comfort me. "And even if you found a way, your grandfather isn't there anymore.

When someone does something against the government, the entire family is usually penalized. Your doctor grandfather has been kicked out, too. Or if he hasn't been kicked out, he's been stripped of all his things and likely left on his own to survive. You'll never find him."

"But what if my grandfather is looking for me?" I looked up, my heart racing as if the electricity had just come on inside me. I knew I had to find him. He would help both my sickness and me.

"Good luck with that, fancy-pants Pyongyang boy. Unless he's looking for you, unless he knows you are here, you won't find him."

"But he would never abandon us. I know that."

"Then how come he hasn't come yet?"

Young-bum was right. We'd been in Gyeong-seong for nearly a year and a half. *Hal-abeoji* hadn't come. I lowered my head, feeling all hope drain, like on a hot steamy day being given a glass of water with holes in it. I swallowed hard so as not to cry.

"Why do you think my mother didn't take me with her?" I asked timidly. Another question I didn't really want the answer to, but I felt I needed to know.

"Because it's too dangerous. She'd have to hitch rides with farmers. She was afraid, as she should be, that you might be caught by the *Shangmoo*."

"*Shangmoo?*"

"You've never heard of the 9.27 *Shangmoo*?" he asked, staring at me wide-eyed. I grunted no. "On September 27, the government formed the *Shangmoo*, a band of police to collect people who are not at home or at school and take them to shelters. Every city has a force of these 9.27 *Shangmoo*, except maybe Pyongyang, because you're like the golden perfect city in the sky, with golden perfect people who all have homes and who never do anything wrong. But everywhere else, there are so many kids not at school, adults hunting for food . . . the *Shangmoo*'s job is to clean the streets of these people. The *Shangmoo* send the people they find to so-called shelters—the adults to one place, the kids to another. But these are not nice places. They're *guhoso*, jails. On the streets, we call the *Shangmoo* the *cleaners*, because that's what they do. They rid Joseon of its dirty people."

"Where are you taking me?" I demanded, afraid he was taking me to the prison. Maybe *he* was one of these so-called cleaners.

"Here," he said, stopping. We were standing at the edge of the market.

"Look," he then said, speaking slowly and softly, as if he were the one in pain, not me, "it's just my grandmother and me now. Aunt lives a few towns away from here, and her husband left for China and never came back, just like our dads. Aunt sells coal, and when she sells enough, she brings food for my grandmother. But that's not often. I have to steal food to sell to buy medicine to keep my grandmother alive. I can't . . . ," he began, then stopped.

"You can't what?"

"I can't look after you. This is your kitchen now," Young-bum said, waving an arm around the market. I followed his hand and looked into the tired eyes of the vendors, eyes that no longer reflected light. The men were wrinkled, sunken, and walking around on bowlegs; the children had runny noses, swollen stomachs, and open sores; the women, who like my own *eomeoni*, I could tell from their fine features and graceful movements, had been beautiful once like swans, until their skin became first pallid from malnutrition and then blue from dirt and their hair began to fall out.

"At least you're alive," Young-bum whispered.

"Am I?" I grunted, then added: "My grandfather, *that grandfather who isn't looking for me*, told me when I was little that our nightmares always seem real. Maybe . . . ," I whispered, but Young-bum didn't hear. He had already left.

I finished my sentence anyway. "Maybe I died a long time ago, and this is just my nightmare."

moved to the side of the market and sat down on a piece of cardboard. I then spent hours thinking, looking out at nothing through dazed, disbelieving eyes, trying to make sense of all that was happening to me. I eventually gave up and focused on the market instead. Almost all the vendors, who had set up tables and were selling goods from dried fish to electronics, were men, often with a woman, perhaps a wife, helping them. Women without men walked around, in and out of the stalls, selling prepared foods, such as fried tofu, twisted bread sticks, and hard-boiled eggs, from baskets they held close.

About midmorning, I spied some boys around my age, but some older. While their clothes were grease-stained, tattered, and dirty like those of the merchants, their skin and hair were healthy. Their bodies were filled out, too, not skeletal. They walked in and out of the market stalls with a confidence that I sure didn't feel.

I studied them closely and saw that they moved around the

market like a wolf pack. One member of the group, a boy not much taller than me, reached up and opened a bag a woman wore draped down her back. Without her knowledge, he slipped his slender fingers inside and withdrew a small pouch.

My eyes trailed the boy as he walked at a normal pace out of the market until he eventually disappeared, heading in the direction of the train station. I turned my attention back to the woman. She still had not noticed she'd been robbed.

It was the aroma of baking bread that lured me to get up and walk around. I made my way behind a small table, on which some fresh bread had been placed underneath a fishing net. Blackflies fought one another on top of the netting.

"Please, may I have one?" I turned to ask the woman. But no words came out. I had never begged before. I lowered my head in shame and blushed. I wanted to tell this woman that I was from Pyongyang, to assure her that if she knew me, I would pay her back if she would feed me now. I wanted her to know that I was a good son, a future general, and that I needed someone to help me, as the Koreans had helped our eternal leader on his childhood march from Manchuria back to his hometown, Mangyeongdae.

She stared at me through lost eyes, waiting, I guess, for me to speak. Instead, I turned and skulked away, back to the side of the market where other boys like me, their faces downcast and their bodies disappearing in their oversize clothes, sat on cardboard boxes or on the bare ground and waited for someone to help them.

People walked in front of me, back and forth. I looked up and into their faces, hoping that someone would give me something to eat. But no one even looked at me. I had never felt so ashamed in my life as I sat there waiting for a handout that never came. At dusk, I gave up, closed my eyes, and prayed silently for Chilseong and *shan-shin-ryong-nim* to help me.

Then I smelled it again: the scent of fresh baked bread, and it was drawing near. I opened my eyes to find the woman standing in front of me, holding out a twisted bun. "Here," she said, pushing it toward me.

"Thank you," I said, trying to pull myself up to bow. But she pushed my shoulders and me back down.

"I want you to leave," she said, kneeling down and leaning in real close. "You're scaring customers away. Don't come back tomorrow, dirty *kotjebi*."

I tried to tell her that I didn't know what a *kotjebi* was. But she was gone, fast, just as Young-bum had left me, turning quickly and escaping back to a safer life than mine.

WHEN NIGHT FELL, BRINGING WITH IT HEAVY CLOUDS AND a cool wind, I looked around for some plastic sheeting I could pull over on top of me to keep me warm. There was nothing. Some of the merchants were from out of town, so they slept in the market. As these merchants lit their fires, I lay my head down on the dusty ground. Tiny pebbles dug their way into my cheeks, but I was too tired and hungry to care. I fell asleep.

About midnight, I felt a sharp kick and then a deep, gruff voice chortled right up and into my ear: "Get out of here."

I pulled open my eyes, which were still swollen and sticky with puss, and stared up into the faces of two old men, both reeking of alcohol and urine. The men began pinching and poking me, telling me to get up. For a few seconds I didn't move. Then I coughed up some phlegm.

"At least he's alive," the huskier of the two men said. The other man was stick-thin, all bones.

"Where is your house?" the bone-man asked. He was now leaning down and feeling my forehead to see if I was sick. I slapped his hand away.

"You can't stay here," he growled. "Go home or else the *Shangmoo* will take you away. Only merchants are allowed to be here at night."

"Just take me to the *guhoso*. Don't wait for the *Shangmoo*," I hissed, tired and fed up.

The men stood back and laughed. "The *guhoso* is a killing field," the skinnier of the two said. "Kids go in and never come out."

"It's full of disease and death," the huskier man said. "Go home . . . go anywhere except stay here. *Kotjebi* can't sleep in this market."

There was that word again. *Kotjebi*. "What does *kotjebi* mean?" I asked, trying to pull myself up. The slimmer of the two men saw me struggling and gave me a hand.

"A *kotjebi* is a boy who lives on the street, stupid," the huskier man snapped. He then pinched my earlobe hard to get me to turn around and start walking away. I planted my feet.

"I'm not a street boy," I mumbled. "My parents have gone away to find food. I am from a good family, party members. Can you help me?"

The men put their hands on their hips and started laughing again. "Every *kotjebi* has the same story," the heavyset man finally said.

"Here is the hierarchy out here," the slim man said. "Army is on the top. You'll only see them if you try to steal from certain government farms. Then the police, followed by the *Shangmoo*. Then there are workers, followed by merchants, followed by you, *kotjebi*. There is only one group of people lower than you."

"What is that?" I asked nervously.

"The nightflowers," he hissed. The two men then started howling and laughing again, loudly, like wolves, a cacophony that moved across the market.

"I have nowhere to go," I said shyly.

The men suddenly stopped laughing. For a moment I felt as if everyone were staring at me, like on the first day of school. Then they started howling again, along with a bunch of other market men.

I staggered away from the men at that point, out of the market and along the gravel road, tripping every so often on my tired feet, as if it were I who was drunk. I was halfway up a small hill, panting, keeling over from nausea and a sharp cramp in my side, not really sure where I was going, when I stopped. There was a bend in the road that overlooked a clearing. I walked up to it and looked down a sharp rock face. *I could fall off here,* I thought. *And die.* "Death will solve all my problems, I whispered out loud.

My feet inched toward the edge of the precipice. I took a deep breath and counted to ten.

But then I couldn't do it. I couldn't jump.

I looked up at the waning moon poking out from behind a rain cloud. "Why?" I yelled as some rays caressed the fields of the government potato farm, the same farm where my mother once worked.

I felt so far away from beauty, stuck in the shadows of a nightmare, unable to find my way into the light.

"*Why?*" I shouted again.

couldn't go back to my house. There was no food. I could die there. Worse, no one would know I was dead, and I wouldn't have a proper burial.

I had no choice. I headed back to the only place I knew.

Young-bum kicked me hard in my left leg when I pushed the door open and fell into his house like a bouncing ball for the second time in less than three days.

"Don't be angry. Don't be cross," I spluttered as I crumpled to the floor. "I've nowhere to go except the *guhoso*, where the men in the market say diseases run rampant."

"I told you that kids die there," he snapped. "Not that you ever listen to me."

"I do, I do! I do now," I pleaded. "Please let me stay here, and I will help you look after your grandmother," I said, thinking fast, hoping to convince Young-bum that if I stayed, I could be an asset. "I'll help you steal."

Young-bum crossed his arms and glared at me. "At least some of your swelling has gone down," he growled at me.

"Look," I pressed on. "I've spent the past day observing the market. The only people who pass through who look at all like they're surviving are the *kotjebi* . . . the *kotjebi* who work in teams. The *kotjebi* who are alone, like me, move like *yu-ryeong*, along the sides . . . We don't have much of a chance, as we're all just waiting for people to help us, and, of course, no one does. But those *kotjebi* who join forces—they seem to thrive. They are strong and healthy. Together we can make a team and care for each other and your grandmother."

Young-bum sighed, threw his hands in the air, and walked to where his grandmother lay. Still looking at me, he lowered his head and whispered something into her ear.

She raised her head and mumbled something back. Young-bum nodded.

"Okay, we'll try," he said to me. I exhaled. "My grandmother says we don't have extra food, so you feed yourself," he continued. "Here's the deal. If we only have enough food for one person, my grandmother comes first, always. Agreed?"

"Yes," I replied with a weak smile.

"There's more," he added. "If you die, I leave you out on the street."

I had no choice. I had to agree to that, too.

¤ ¤ ¤

"I KNOW WHAT YOU'RE SAYING ABOUT FORMING A TEAM . . .
a gang," Young-bum said the next morning as we shared the
last remaining potato, which we ate with a broth he had made
from dandelion roots. "I joined a gang after my mother died. The
Jjacdari-pa gang. My gang taught me how to steal, but I got beaten
up. That's how I lost my tooth—remember?—and kicked out for
keeping some of the money I stole for myself. I was supposed
to share everything with them. That is the gang rule. I needed
the money to buy my grandmother's pills. Look." He pulled out
a small leather pouch from his back pocket. He placed it on the
ground and slowly spread it open. Inside was a *ring-nal*, a razor
blade, like the one my father used to shave himself.

"Where did you get that?" I gasped. Since we arrived in
Gyeong-seong, razors were hard to find. My father had shaved
with a sharp knife.

"Stole it . . . when I was part of the gang." Young-bum picked it
up. "*Woosh woosh*," he said as he flung it through the air. "I go up
behind women in the market, cut a small hole in their bags, and
steal their wallets and purses."

I thought of the *kotjebi* I'd seen at the market stealing. I then
thought of the woman he stole from. When I put a face to the victim, my heart sank. "Young-bum," I whispered. "The people *kotjebi* steal from are starving, too. They might have children at home
like us. They could be mothers—our mothers—and by stealing
from them, their own children might go hungry."

Young-bum fell quiet. "If I think about that, I'll die," he finally said in a contemplative tone. "Morality is a great song a person sings when he or she has never been hungry. You can walk the noble road, Sungju. But if you die because of it, nobody will remember you were a noble person. Just a fool. Our enemy is death now. You know how Kim Il-sung said that children are the kings and queens of the nation?" he asked.

"Yeah."

"I think this is not true. If it were true, we wouldn't be starving."

"You shouldn't say such things about the regime," I warned, still fearful of defying my government, including by speaking bad about it in public.

Young-bum laughed. "This is why those fat cats in Pyongyang liked you so much," he said, tickling me. "You're a coward. You're . . . What's the word? Compliant. Easy. If your life hadn't taken a different turn, you would have made a perfect general. You'd do whatever they asked of you, without thinking twice."

I stared at him for the longest time, my face growing hot as anger bubbled up inside me. He was right, of course. Even now, if my government asked me to do something, I would do it. I'm not sure exactly with whom I was most upset: Young-bum or the regime.

Young-bum stopped smiling. "Look, those Pyongyang people care only about their own power," he continued. "You were being raised to be one of their military officers, not because you were good but because you obeyed. But whether you saw it or not, your job, if you had been successful in becoming a general, would have been to protect their interests, no doubt about it. And one of their interests is to suppress people like me."

I didn't want to think anymore. I had a pounding headache.

"Let's go to the market," I said with a sigh. "Let's just get on with it."

I SKIRTED AROUND VENDORS AND THE WOMEN HAWKING their steamed bread and candies, struggling to follow Young-bum through the market. He was very quick on his feet.

At midmorning, when the market was at its most crowded and the din of people bartering over prices was at its loudest, Young-bum stopped and flicked his fingers, indicating for me to stand back. I did and then followed him with my eyes. He was on the tail of a middle-aged woman carrying a plate of steaming buns. A fabric bag, similar to my own and stitched together from old clothes, was slung over her shoulders and fell low by her side.

I didn't move as Young-bum stalked her like a wolf does a wapiti. When he was right behind her, he used that double-bladed razor to slice a hole in the front of her bag. He then slipped his slender fingers into the bag and drew out some contents, including a small purse. He then spun around on his heels and walked back toward me. As he passed me, he didn't make eye contact, but I could see the corners of his lips go up in a weak smile. He kept right on walking like the other *kotjebi* thief had, out of the market, nonchalantly, as if he hadn't just stolen from someone.

My mouth watered looking around at all the food: dried pollack from the East Sea, kimchi laid out in paper bowls, and rice cakes with sesame seeds, the aroma of which made me remember my recurring dream of *abeoji*'s return from China. I soon started to feel weak again, this time not from my illness but from hunger. I'd learned something about hunger in the past year. After a certain point, I didn't feel it as a burning ache anymore. Rather, my body just didn't do what I asked it to do.

I slapped my cheeks to stop myself from passing out. "Get a grip," I scolded myself. I took a few deep breaths to get the energy moving through me. I then imitated Young-bum's steady, swift walk through the market, confident, as if I were either selling or buying, not about to steal. I approached an older, toothless man displaying electrical wires. On the table, off to the side, were candies placed in small envelopes.

The man was engrossed in fixing what looked like a radio. I moved toward his table as if I were just passing by.

He didn't look up. He didn't even notice me.

Not even slowing down, I slid my hand out to the side and whisked the candies into the pockets of my pants, Young-bum's old school uniform. I didn't turn around to see if the man had seen. I kept moving, not fast, just steady, to where I had spent most of my first day at the market; the cardboard I had sat on still remained on the ground. I bent over to collect my breath and steady my nerves, all the while scanning the crowd for my next victim.

The woman who had given me the bun and told me I was *kot-jebi* was at the same spot.

I started to move toward her, hoping now that my swelling had gone down a bit, she wouldn't recognize me. As my luck would have it, just as I reached her table, another woman approached her to buy some eggs. I snuck around the back as the two women argued over the price. I lifted the netting with the flies gripping the top, grabbed three buns, and stuffed them into the fold of my shirt.

I was nearly back to the cardboard box on the ground when I felt a heavy hand come down on my back, nearly knocking the wind out of me. The hand spun me around quickly, making me feel dizzy. I looked up and into the cold stare of a middle-aged man with salt-and-pepper hair. He wrapped his long crooked fingers around my throat. "Put them back," he said, sticking his foul-smelling mouth up close to my face.

I shook my head no.

His fingers dug hard into my flesh, and I felt my feet lifting off the ground. I saw stars and moving lights, and I began to gag. I heard the sound of running feet and then saw the female vendor's face and her wild, bloodshot eyes. She slapped at me with her calloused hands, ripping into my bare skin. I knew I was about to black out from lack of air when all of a sudden a force grew up from inside me. I saw myself not in the market but facing my tae kwon do master.

I kicked the man in his groin and then butted his head hard against mine. He tumbled backward, letting go of me as he fell to the ground. I started to trip, too, but I quickly found my footing, jumped up, and kicked the woman in the stomach. She fell backward and to the ground, too.

I then walked out of the market toward Ha-myeon Bridge, looking back as I did to make sure I wasn't being followed.

13

W hile I held a damp cloth, which I had dipped in the river, on the swollen nose I got from head-butting the man, Young-bum discussed strategies for my stealing the next time around. The first rule was to never return to the same safe spot, which I had done when I went back to the cardboard box. He criticized me. "Merchants know where you're headed when you do that. Go toward the train station. After you steal, walk normally, as if you haven't done anything wrong, and surround yourself with lots of people."

As we talked, another idea came to me, which I told Young-bum after he finished laying into me about my mistakes.

The next day, when we headed to the market, we decided to try it to see if it would work.

At midmorning, when the market was at its busiest, Young-bum and I sauntered up close behind a woman who had a bag slung over her shoulder. Young-bum cut a hole in the bottom of her sack—not on the side, as he had been doing. The contents of the woman's bag fell into his own, contents that included not just her wallet or small purse but also small packages of food. I then slipped a brick into the woman's bag and fastened the fabric back together with safety pins ever so carefully so she wouldn't feel any pressure and catch me in the act. The victim, who was talking to a vendor, didn't even catch on that she'd been robbed.

"It works," I whispered as we crossed Ha-myeon Bridge. I felt both pride as well as sadness at our success, for I was now a thief, having stolen not just a piece of bread but won.

Young-bum glowed like the sun. "It really does! Now I can take twice as much, if not three or four times more than I ever could before. We'll be rich!" he said, jumping up and down as I had done at my birthday parties in Pyongyang when *eomeoni* served cake. "We can eat the food and sell what we don't need. You're brilliant!"

"So . . . we're a team, then?" I asked, holding my hand out for him to shake.

"We're a team," he said, taking it.

EVERY EVENING FOR THE NEXT FEW MONTHS, AFTER Young-bum and I had finished at the market, he returned to his home to feed his grandmother. I went to my own house to check in, hoping—no, daydreaming—that when I opened the door, *eomeoni* would be there, praying over her bowl of fresh well water. Every day, though, I'd find the house empty, growing lonelier, like an abandoned amusement park, hollow and haunted like some of the people I'd see in the market. The house was collecting dust, cobwebs, a family of field mice, and lots of cockroaches.

Every day, Young-bum and I stole twisted bread sticks, candies, *dububab*, and won. With the won, we bought his grandmother's medicine and then white rice and soybean paste, which he would cook into meals for his grandmother. With all the food she was now eating and the proper doses of medicine she was getting, her health slowly improved. By the start of harvest season, she started spending her days sitting up, and soon she was standing. By the middle of the fall, she'd even awake before Young-bum and me and prepare us a meal of corn rice and vegetable porridge. As we'd eat, she'd tell us stories about what Joseon was like before Kim Il-sung. "It was a terrible time when the Japanese made slaves of us all. If you think now is tough . . . ," she would always say, ending her sentence by clicking her tongue: "*Tsk, tsk.*" While she didn't come right out and say it, Young-bum and I both knew she was saying we should bear our hardships the way our eternal leader had borne his. Hunker down like Kim Il-sung did in the *Learning Journey of a Thousand Miles.*

Young-bum and I pretended to listen, but we'd heard enough of these stories in school. "The past doesn't feed us," Young-bum would say as we'd walk the road to the market.

I realized after spending nearly all my time with Young-bum that when he had chanted for the prisoners to be executed, he wasn't doing so because he believed they should be killed. He was putting on a show so the principal and the *so-nyon-dan* manager wouldn't think he was a criminal, too. Truth: I don't think Young-bum believed in anything anymore, least of all in Joseon. He believed in survival, plain and simple. His grandmother's and his own.

I was in the middle somewhere between them, trying to find my way out of a murky bog, no longer believing in a lot that our eternal leader, his son, or our country had ever told me, but also not wanting to believe yet that life was the survival of the strongest street boy. I wanted to believe in my mother's prayer bowl, in Chilseong, *shan-shin-ryong-nim* . . . that something higher and good was also at play.

THE HARVEST MOON CAME AND WENT. AS THE COOLER weather moved around us, Young-bum and I began to worry about the winter. We both felt we should try to steal more money and more vegetables to store in his grandmother's underground cooler, as well as blankets and firewood. Young-bum suggested we pick the pockets of passengers at the train station, from the few people who still had jobs and earned won. "The people working will certainly have more won than those poor women at the market," he said. "We should try."

At first, I resisted the idea, fearful of running into a *kotjebi* gang, like the one I'd watched on my very first day in the market. I didn't want to get beat up as Young-bum had.

"I'm afraid, too," Young-bum replied when I voiced my concern. "My old gang, the *Jjacdari-pa*, worked out of the train station, and yeah, if they saw me there stealing, they'd try to kill me. They've moved on to another city, though—at least, the last I heard. I think we're safe. I promise if I see any of my former gang members . . ."

I had stopped listening. Something was playing over and over again in my mind. "Young-bum," I finally interrupted him, "what do you think about you and me joining a gang? I mean, if we formed our own gang, found some other *kotjebi*, and made our own rules, then we'd be in control."

Young-bum looked at me as if it were Kim Il-sung's birthday and pork was being rationed out to everyone. He patted me on the back. "Great idea. I may even know the guys who can do this with us," he said with a grin.

WE HEADED STRAIGHT TO THE TRAIN STATION'S WAITING room. There were about two hundred people, true enough, but most of them were *degeori*, merchants who sold their goods from town to town, and other *kotjebi*. The merchants were just as poor as we were, and we *kotjebi* gave each other the evil eye, hoping to intimidate one another. A few of the harder, bigger *kotjebi* belted their fists into the palms of their hands, indicating they wanted to fight Young-bum and me. They'd make a move as if they were about to pounce on us, but then the police would arrive to check the room. The policemen's ice-cold eyes would linger on each *kotjebi*. While no words were exchanged, I knew what the police were thinking: *Try anything, steal, fight . . . and off to the guhoso you will go.*

As morning slipped its way into the afternoon, Young-bum's patience began to wear. He started to pace back and forth and sigh. Finally, he took a deep breath and bravely approached one of the police officers, asking when the train was due in. The officer looked away, wanting nothing to do with him, which was better than his wanting to arrest Young-bum.

Young-bum pressed on, however, explaining that he was waiting for his grandmother, who was coming in on the next train. "I'm not like these other boys," Young-bum said to the man, his eyes moving around the room. "I think they're *kotjebi*," he whispered, and then scrunched up his face, as if he had just eaten something sour. "I just want to see my grandmother and take her to my mother, who is sick."

"You'll have a long wait," the officer snapped, and then stormed off without giving an explanation.

We were still waiting when the room grew darker and the cream marble floor became streaked in long shadows. Twilight had begun to wrap itself around us.

I was frustrated now, too, with no food or money to show for our day.

Just as I was about to drag Young-bum out of there and to the market to at least find some bread sticks for dinner, the policeman with whom Young-bum had spoken moved to the center of the room. He cupped his hands together to act as a bullhorn and announced that the train wasn't coming today. "There's no electricity," he said. "The train is stuck somewhere between Kimchaek and Gilju."

I kicked Young-bum hard in the shin. "This was such a bad idea," I said with a scowl, watching as the crowd of *kotjebi* began to disperse. If we didn't hurry, they'd get to the market before us and steal whatever was still out, leaving us and Young-bum's grandmother hungry.

We took a shortcut, heading along the platform to try to get to the market before the other *kotjebi*. As we neared the end, I heard "The sound of thunder at Jong-Il peak" lines from the *Boy General* song, sung by that voice with the cascading falsetto that I knew belonged to Sangchul.

Young-bum and I pushed our way through the crowd that had gathered around Sangchul on the grassy knoll at the end of the platform, a crowd full of odors of unclean clothes, hair, and bodies. When we reached the front, we could see Sangchul standing in the middle of this circle of people. Min-gook and two boys I recognized from our class but whose names I didn't know were collecting won and food from the audience.

"That's Myeongchul and Unsik," Young-bum whispered to me. "Sangchul and Myeongchul are street performers. They put on plays and sing songs. Myeongchul is the actor. He won competitions in theater."

"Did you know they were here?"

"I thought they might be here," he hummed. He then turned, started tapping his foot, and looked at me with wide eyes.

"Are we thinking the same thing?" I asked.

"I hope so," he said with a twinkle in his eye.

"Here's our gang!"

14

The six of us sat on the ground with our backs against the chipped stone wall, facing the empty platform. We had just gone to the market with the money they'd earned performing and bought a dinner of noodles made from corn as well as some food for Young-bum's grandmother.

Night had now fallen, and all around us were drunken men and a few women. The men would shout at one another, slurring their words. The women skulked around and asked in hushed voices: "Anyone want a nightflower? A nightflower?"

I made a mental note to ask Young-bum what *nightflower* meant, as this was the second time I'd heard the word.

Sangchul and the others didn't seem to care about the chaos around them. We began to talk about our parents. Those who hadn't died were missing, having gone in search of food like my mother and father. The boys had found a way to earn enough money to buy food by performing on the street. Myeongchul, who took over the talking from Sangchul, explained that he put on skits based on Kim Il-sung's books. After Myeongchul performed, Sangchul would sing, usually partisan songs such as "We Are Kid Scouts."

> *"We are brave because we're kid scouts.*
> *Even though there are storms out there blocking us,*
> *we are brave.*
> *We pay back our enemies, a thousand times . . ."*

We all sang together.

Min-gook and Unsik were the heavies, as Myeongchul described them, collecting money from the spectators. The boys all slept at the train station in the waiting room when it was really cold or outside when it was warmer.

"Chulho thinks our fathers are stuck in China," Myeongchul said.

"Chulho thinks they'll come back in the winter," Sangchul jumped in, "when the river turns to ice and it's too cold for the guards to be out for long and our parents can run across the river, rather than swim."

Chulho, Chulho, Chulho. He might not have been there in person, but he sure didn't feel that far away, either. "Where is the infamous Chulho?" I finally cut in.

"Ah, he's mushroom hunting," Myeongchul said with a laugh. "He's somewhere in the hills, picking the government's prized mushrooms and selling them to smugglers who take them into China to sell. Chulho has seen and done it all."

"Chulho told us that most adults now need permits to take trains, even for single stops, and the government isn't giving out many anymore," Sangchul added. "Kids, of course, have to be with their parents and have their birth certificates on them all the time to prove that their parents really are their parents. So I figure my parents are stuck right where they are, waiting for permits."

"Yeah," I said wistfully, looking off into the flames of a fire that some men were tending near the grassy knoll where Sangchul sang earlier in the day. "I bet my mom is waiting for a permit." I could see her now in my mind's eye, stuck in Wonsan with Aunt Nampo, waiting to return to me. Instead of focusing on my own suffering, I realized for the first time that *eomeoni* must be worried sick about me.

I left Young-bum and the others as they arranged to meet again the next day and ran at full speed back to my house, making a list as I went of all the chores I wanted to do, including sweeping the cobwebs away and scrubbing the dust that had caked the floor. I'd spend the night, and in the morning I would wash the few remaining blankets and sheets. When *eomeoni* returned, the house would sparkle. I wanted her to be proud of me.

¤ ¤ ¤

WHEN I TURNED THE CORNER AND MY HOUSE CAME INTO view, I stopped. There was a light streaming out from the front window. My hands started to shake, and my heart pounded. "*Eomeoni* and *abeoji* are home!" I exclaimed out loud.

I crept toward the door, staring at the light, afraid that if I looked away, I'd discover it to be just a dream.

As I stepped into the house, a gust of warm air from the cooking fire rolled over me. "*Eomeoni?*" I called out.

Silence.

I looked around the room, at blankets I didn't recognize piled in one corner, tin bowls we didn't have scattered on top of a new table and shoes lined up on the mat, including several pairs of men's sneakers and two pairs of women's slippers. I blinked and felt so happy inside. "My parents are home, and they've come with lots of new things."

When I opened my eyes, though, instead of seeing *eomeoni* and *abeoji*, I was staring at the bewildered faces of two men, one my father's age, the other my grandfather's age. A middle-aged woman emerged from the back room, gripping hard the hands of two small children, a girl and a boy. In their free hands, each child was holding a children's story written by Kim Il-sung.

"Who are you?" I demanded.

"Who are *you?*" the older man with graying hair said, taking a giant step toward me. His tone of voice was forceful but not unkind.

"I—I—I live here," I stammered.

The man replied, "Son, this house is ours. We bought it."

I clenched my fists and bit my lip to stop myself from crying. "This is *my* house," I said. "I . . ." I stopped suddenly. There was no more echo. The house now had things—but not my family's things. "Where are my family's belongings?" I asked.

"There wasn't much," the woman said in a sympathetic voice.

"But where are those *few* things?" I demanded.

"They've been sold," the older man said.

"You sold my things!" I exclaimed. My mind ran over all the items that were special, that I wanted, including my mother's wedding chest and her photographs.

"Where?" I said, my voice now hoarse. "Where were they sold?" *Eomeoni*'s prayer bowl. I wanted that, too. And her bedding. It might still smell like her. Thoughts crashed into my mind like metal shovels hitting concrete.

"We don't know," the older man continued. "The *binjibpali* took it all away."

"*Binjibpali?*" I asked, puzzled. I'd never heard that word before, like *kotjebi* and *nightflower*.

"The broker said that it was his house and that the items belonged to him. *Binjibpali* is a person who finds empty houses like this and then sells them," the woman explained. "But in this case, the man said this was his house."

I looked down. I hadn't done a good job at holding back my

tears. They now stained my shirt, Young-bum's white button-down shirt that once had been his school uniform. "You have to get out," I said under my breath. "My parents are coming home soon. I want to clean for them."

The younger man now moved toward me. "No," he said sternly. His speech was spitting, like Chulho's. I stepped back from the force.

"We're not leaving." He faced me squarely, clenching his fists. "This is not your house, not anymore. We bought it from the owners. Now get out. And pretend you never even came here."

"I can't do that," I said, looking pleadingly into his eyes, hoping that I could get through to this man that *this was my house.*

This man, though, was colder than the police officers at the Gyeong-seong train station earlier that day.

"We have papers," he continued, "papers that say we bought this house legally."

I shook my head slowly. "But th-th-there's been a mistake," I said, stuttering again. My head throbbed. I felt both hot and cold at the same time.

The younger man started pushing me toward the door. "Get out," he spat. "Don't make us call the *Shangmoo* and have you thrown in prison."

"How . . . ," I began, my voice quivering. "How will my parents find me if I'm not here?" I tried to push back, but I didn't have the strength.

The man grabbed the collar of my shirt with one hand, and with the other my waist, and heaved me out the open door. I landed on my stomach on the hard ground. He then slammed the door shut, locking it behind him.

I COULD FEEL THE *YU-RYEONG*, WHO I KNEW THRIVED IN lonely places, including those parts inside us, breathing down hard on me, making the hairs on the back of my neck stand on end, as I walked up the road toward the forest where my father and I had hunted chipmunks and snakes.

I turned onto the dirt path leading into the woods. It was dark under the canopy of evergreen boughs and leaves, almost pitch-black the farther I went into the forest, in part because of the moonless night and the clouds rolling in. My feet sank into the mud of a shallow swamp, letting me know I had taken a turn off the path. Branches of evergreen trees ensnarled me, and burrs dug their way into my clothes and scratched my skin.

My body felt heavy. My head spun. I eventually collapsed beside a large oak tree and fell asleep.

I was awakened sometime in the middle of the night by the throaty call of a wood owl. I started to tremble from the chill of the mist moving up from the river and the dampness that seeped up from the ground. I also tingled all over from the feeling that I was not alone.

My father had told me once that owls guarded the realm where the spirits of our ancestors now lived. I curled my body into a tight ball, my back flush against the knots of the tree trunk, and listened to the night walk of beetles and bugs.

Then I saw it. Tiny, floating soft blue and warm white lights hovering in front of me. I strained my eyes, at first thinking these were fireflies. But then I saw they weren't. They seemed to be attached to the trunk of a decaying tree that stood near me. I felt wind brushing my cheek, and the lights moved with the breeze, like a feather on top of a calm river.

"Is that you, *shan-shin-ryong-nim*?" I whispered.

My body stiffened as the sounds of the forest faded, replaced by an almost celestial silence and then the sound of distant bells.

I was dead. I had died. There was no other explanation, I thought to myself.

I exhaled and relaxed, knowing that if I were dead, there would be nothing to worry about anymore.

I tilted my head up toward the top of the tree and prayed to Chilseong.

"Please watch over *eomeoni* and *abeoji*. I know they're alive," I said out loud. "If I do manage to survive this place of the dead, have my family look for me, reunite me with them. Let us be one again. Guide me."

When I opened my eyes, I saw shadows around me. Day was beginning to win its battle against night.

¤ ¤ ¤

A LIGHT DRIZZLE SOON PATTED MY FACE. IGNORING MY sore joints and aching back, and with an energy I certainly didn't have the night before, I hopped up and ran back through the ferns, swamp, and thornbushes to the road and then to Young-bum's house.

I barged through the front door, huffing and excited, just as he was preparing to get an early start at the market.

"I . . . I . . . ," I spluttered. I wanted to tell him about the lights, about *shan-shin-ryong-nim*. But as I stood in front of him, I changed my mind.

"Spit it out," Young-bum said. He sounded annoyed. "I thought you were meeting us at the train station, not coming here first."

"I changed my mind," I told him. "I changed my mind about everything. I want to live," I exclaimed, throwing my arms into the air.

Young-bum tilted his head to the side and eyed me suspiciously. "Have you been drinking *sool* with the men?"

"Nahhh . . . Just forget it," I chortled, waving him off. "You wouldn't understand."

Young-bum's grandmother shuffled up beside me and handed me a piece of candy. "*I* understand," she whispered. I looked into her eyes, which had a blue-gray smoky coat over the irises. Young-bum said she was suffering from an eye disease that a lot of old people in the countryside had. As a result of the eye disease, she couldn't see that well. I took the candy from her and bowed.

"My grandmother is going to stay with Aunt in Shang-gi-ryeong," Young-bum said as he slipped the pouch containing his razor blade into the front pocket of his bag. He then poured fresh well water into a dented tin bottle that he and I would drink from throughout the day.

"Have a good trip," I said to Young-bum's grandmother, who wouldn't stop looking at me. "Are you okay?" I finally asked her. Her intense gaze was making me feel uncomfortable.

She smiled. "I'm perfect," she said, her voice raspy, still heavy with fluid.

She then turned her stare to Young-bum. "I have something for you." She shuffled up beside him.

She passed him a package, what looked like an envelope, which he slipped into his back pocket. Then she whispered into his ear. Young-bum's eyelids drooped, and his lips trembled the way I'd seen them do when he was scared.

"Go," his grandmother said to both of us, grinning and gesturing for us to leave. "See you in Shang-gi-ryeong," she called out from the doorway as she pushed us out.

FOR A WHILE, YOUNG-BUM WAS SILENT. HE WALKED WITH his head down, his shoulders slumped, breathing heavily, as if he were carrying a great weight. I whistled "*Dondolari*," my mother's favorite folk song, as I watched some black kites swoop over the harvested fields.

127

"What is it?" I finally asked. I was annoyed at his moroseness when I was so happy.

"I don't think my grandmother is coming back," he said in a quiet voice.

"Maybe it will be better for her at your aunt's house. We can visit her, and you can stay there, too, I'm sure."

"No," he said, stopping and pulling me to the side of the road. He sat down cross-legged on the ground and had me do the same. He then laid out the items from the envelope his grandmother had given him: photographs of people who I assumed were his mother, father, grandmother, and aunt.

"My grandmother said that if she and I didn't see each other again, she wanted me to have these," Young-bum said, floating a hand over the pictures. "She said she wanted me to be strong and look at these when I felt weak."

I had been sailing that day, but now I was sinking again. All I could think about as Young-bum droned on was that I wished I had photographs of my family, too.

persuaded Young-bum to turn around and go to Shang-gi-ryeong with his grandmother. "She's not going to die," I repeated several times, and while Young-bum seemed reassured, by the time we parted ways he was eager to be with her.

"You're going to be the *srikoon* today," he said with a laugh, handing me the leather pouch with the razor in the front pocket.

"A *srikoon*?"

"Yeah, a *kotjebi* who steals by cutting open someone else's bag. Didn't you know that's what I was?" Young-bum chortled.

"I think all these words are make-believe. *Srikoon*, *kotjebi*, *nightflower* . . . ," I said, ruffling his hair.

He winked. "On the street, we have names for everything. Good luck," he called over his shoulder. "I don't want to return to find I have to break you out of the *guhoso*."

¤ ¤ ¤

I WENT TO THE TRAIN STATION TO SEE THE BOYS, AND WHEN I rounded the bend in the road, I found them all sitting on the chipped concrete stairs leading up to the platform. As I neared, I saw that their hair was tousled, like their clothes, and their eyes were glossy and red, as if they'd just woken up. Min-gook was stretching his legs, while Unsik and Sangchul brushed off dirt and sand from each other's shirts.

"It's always darkest under the lamp," Myeongchul announced when he saw me.

I cocked an eyebrow. "What?"

"Old Korean proverb meaning it always looks brighter somewhere else."

"And how does that pertain to me?" I quipped.

"I bet you thought we had a great life," he replied with a laugh. "But see . . . things aren't so great." He held up one of his legs to reveal a big tear in the side seam of his pants. "I got this being chased by a *Shangmoo* who thought I was homeless."

"You are homeless." I laughed. "And you like proverbs!"

"And folk stories and myths, too," he replied with a wide smile. "They say a lot about a culture."

"And what do Korean proverbs say about us?"

"Hmm," he said, scratching his chin. "That we're not airy-fairy whimsical. We're very practical. And we're very hard workers."

"Okay," I replied. "Maybe. Hey, I meant to ask you yesterday. Why do you all sleep in the train station? Why don't you go to your homes?" I asked no one in particular as I sat down on the steps.

"Because other people live in our houses now," Sangchul answered. "Brokers sold our places to other people."

"Mine, too," I whispered, shaking my head and biting my lip as it started to quiver. I was thinking of *eomeoni* returning to find someone else in her house.

Myeongchul stood up and spread out his arms as if hugging the sun. "People are waiting for my acting, followed by Sangchul's fantabulouso singing," he announced in a deep, manlike character voice, like Cheokcheok-hal-abeoji, who narrated the stories of Kim Il-sung's childhood on TV. Sangchul stood up, slipped off his dusty loafers, and banged them against one of the concrete steps to remove some sand and small pebbles.

"Make way for the greatest singer. He's nearly ready!" Min-gook shouted.

People started handing Min-gook and Unsik money as Myeongchul and Sangchul walked toward the grassy knoll by the platform. "People pay," Unsik leaned over and whispered, "just to be in the front row to watch them. You know, both Sangchul and Myeongchul were invited to perform at the Mangyeongdae Children's Palace in Pyongyang."

"Did they go?"

"No. They both had to stay here to make won for their families." Then he added, "Dreams are only for Pyongyang people."

Overhearing, Myeongchul snapped: "You only dream when you sleep. We must reap what we've sewn in daylight. You watch!"

As he stepped into the middle of a circle that was forming around him, he called out, "I'm tilling the land right now for great things to happen!" He did a few steps of the shoulder dance. "The greatest art is born from adversity."

"He certainly is happy," I mused.

"He's just a fool with all his sayings," Unsik said with a sigh. "One day he'll take those blinders off his eyes and see the truth of his life."

"I think, when we stop dreaming, we're just as good as dead," I said in such a hushed voice Unsik didn't hear, which was fine by me.

Myeongchul's skit that day was about the brothers Heungbu and Nolbu. Next, Sangchul sang "We Are Kid Scouts" followed by "Let's Make Impregnable Village." When the applause for their performances had died down, but the audience remained clapping for an encore, Sangchul dragged me into the center of the circle.

"Here is the best tae kwon do performer in the country," he announced, pointing to me. "If you want to see him do very difficult kicks, donate five won to us."

"No," I protested. I hadn't done any tae kwon do patterns since I left Pyongyang. "I'm not prepared," I said, trying to move back into the crowd. But Sangchul grabbed my arm and pulled me back.

Min-gook waved a fistful of five-won notes that the audience had given him to watch me perform.

I took a deep breath.

I settled my scattered thoughts by focusing on the spot in between, but directly behind, my eyes. I then did the jump front kick, followed by the back side kick, then the jump side kick, and finally the jump turn kick. For a few seconds, I actually forgot where I was. I felt I was in a place where time didn't exist. When I neared the end of my patterns, I heard the *swoosh, swoosh* of my hands and legs slicing through the air.

When done, I bowed to such a huge applause that my ears pounded. I blushed at the attention but was also pleased, for I had found something else I could do to earn won other than be a *srikoon*.

"JOIN US," SANGCHUL SAID AS WE SAUNTERED TO THE market to buy some food with the won we'd all just earned.

"Well, I . . . I . . . I . . . actually . . . hmm," I hemmed and hawed.

"Why not?" Myeongchul asked. "And Young-bum can join us, too, if that's what you're worried about. We'd never leave him behind."

"Actually, Young-bum and I were going to ask all of you if you wanted to join us," I said with a chuckle. "You know, form a gang together."

"There are no original ideas," Myeongchul said, patting me on the back. "At least two people somewhere in the world are think-ing the same thing at the same time."

"So it's a done deal!" Unsik exclaimed.

I nodded. I then explained to them that Young-bum was caring for his sick grandmother and that he and I had to buy medicines and steal food for her, too. I also told them that Young-bum and I would sleep at his house, not at the train station. "Young-bum needs to be near his grandmother when she comes home from Shang-gi-ryeong," I said. "Her lungs sound like a forest stream, and she coughs up blood."

"I know this disease, tuberculosis. We all know someone who has died from it," Myeongchul said with a groan.

"It is the sickness of the poor and weak," Sangchul added.

We grew quiet after that, eventually spreading out when we reached the market to buy fried bread sticks and candies.

After we ate, we returned to the train station and performed three more times that day. At the end of the day, as we watched the sun set, I counted my share. I had earned more won than on my best days stealing with Young-bum. I decided to walk to Shang-gi-ryeong to tell Young-bum about our new gang.

IT WAS NEARING MIDNIGHT WHEN I REACHED THE OUT-skirts of Shang-gi-ryeong. I could tell by the position of the moon and Ursa Major, or Chilseong.

Shang-gi-ryeong was a strange town. A slate film, visible even in the night, coated everything. Young-bum had told me Shang-gi-ryeong was a coal town, which explained the thick, dark cloud that it seemed to sit in. When I turned onto the main street, I stopped and looked up at a large mural of Kim Il-sung, which like the one in Gyeong-seong, was clean, like a lily floating in a bog. Lit by the moon, I could read some of the red lettering underneath: OUR GREAT LEADER IS ALWAYS WITH US.

"Indeed, he is," I whispered out loud.

There was no sign of life; no bike against the side of a house, no rake, no broom, not even a candle set in the windowsill of one of the houses.

Young-bum's aunt lived in a brick house off the third road to the right past the mural. I counted my steps out loud because I wanted to hear my own voice, to remind me I was still in the world of the living.

Young-bum's aunt's place wasn't difficult to find; it was the only building that had a light coming from inside.

I knocked on the door, and it creaked open. Young-bum was sitting on the floor, hunched over, rocking back and forth and gripping the gray scarf his grandmother had worn around her neck when she was sick. I started to move toward him to take it, in case it contained her disease and made Young-bum sick, too. I then stopped.

Young-bum didn't look up, and he didn't need to tell me. His grandmother had died.

I bent down and pulled him into my arms, the way my *eomeoni* had done when I scraped a knee or bruised an elbow. He buried his head in my shoulder, and we both cried like newborn babies.

I fought hard not to feel my own pain, but I couldn't. I missed *eomeoni* and *abeoji*. I couldn't avoid that ache inside me that was harder to bear than even hunger. We were alone now. Our loved ones had left, taking a big hole out of us with them when they departed. At twelve years old, I now had to look after myself. I had no one to rely on to guide me to make the best decisions for my life. I had no one to come home to who would hold me and make me feel the world was safe.

"It was her heart," Young-bum coughed out. "My grand-mother's heart just stopped."

"When?" I asked.

"Within a few hours of her arriving here. She just collapsed on the ground, and Aunt and I couldn't wake her."

FOR THE NEXT THREE DAYS I STAYED CLOSE TO YOUNG-BUM while Sangchul, Min-gook, Unsik, and Myeongchul worked harder than ever, performing twice as much as they usually did, to earn won to give Young-bum's grandmother a proper funeral. This included greeting all mourners with dishes of food such as fried tofu with vegetable side dishes and *sool*.

Young-bum's aunt, Mi Shun, and I set up the funeral table in the center of the main room. On top of it, Mi Shun placed a photograph of Young-bum's grandmother, her wedding picture, in which she wore a traditional dress with *Strobilanthes oligantha* made from white tissue paper in her hair. Her cheeks, I could tell even in the black-and-white photo, had been powdered until they were white like snow. She looked beautiful.

Not many mourners came. Mi Shun told me Shang-gi-ryeong had recently had a coal-mining accident in which many workers had died. Lots of families were left without fathers, she said, and the widows moved to other towns in search of work and food. Those few who remained were mostly the old and too frail to travel. They now dug the earth for coal, which they sold at the markets.

The few mourners who did come placed below Young-bum's grandmother's picture a small white envelope containing a few won, which Mi Shun used to pay the neighbors to make a wooden coffin.

On the morning of the third day, we boys, a neighbor, and Mi Shun placed Young-bum's grandmother in the casket and then the casket in a wheelbarrow, which we pushed to the foot of a nearby mountain. We found some land overlooking the Gyeong-seong River that hadn't been used as a grave yet and dug a hole in the earth, using metal spades. Mi Shun burned the few belongings Young-bum's grandmother had, including her clothes and wedding chest. As I placed rice and kimchi around the grave so that Young-bum's grandmother would have food in the afterlife, I remembered something else about Pyongyang. I had asked my mother after we visited Mansudae Hill after Kim Il-sung's death where we went when we died.

"The afterlife," she replied, "where there is no fear, no hunger, no sickness."

I was glad, as I bowed the customary three times, that Young-bum's grandmother was going to that place.

WE RETURNED TO YOUNG-BUM'S HOUSE IN GYEONG-SEONG, and just as all of us boys, who were now living there, were talking, Chulho showed up carrying a bouquet of wilting orange osmanthus, which he said he got from a smuggler crossing the Duman River. "For your grandmother's grave," he said, handing them to Young-bum. "I'm sorry they're not white," he said so politely I was startled for a moment. I had never heard Chulho be soft or kind before. "And these are also for you," he continued, handing Young-bum a small white paper box.

Perhaps surprised, too, at Chulho's sudden gentleness, Young-bum opened the box slowly and with shaking hands, as if expecting something like a snake to pop out.

When he peered in at the contents, his face opened into a wide grin. He squealed and jumped up and down.

We huddled around him and looked, too. Inside were moon cakes.

"Where did you get these?" I asked, stepping away.

"In China, cakes like these are sold at bake shops," he replied. "Can you believe it? The Chinese eat cake every day!"

Young-bum passed around the box. We each picked out a moon cake to eat.

"They have so much food in China they give rice with pork and chicken to their dogs to fatten them up to eat," Chulho continued, sitting down and uncorking a bottle of *sool* that had been left over from Mi Shun's house. He then started drinking it right from the bottle.

"What are you going to do next?" Myeongchul asked, sitting down beside Chulho. Chulho passed him a cigarette, which Myeongchul lit and smoked.

I looked on with disbelieving eyes. Boys don't drink alcohol or smoke.

Chulho shrugged. "I don't know what I'll do next," he said, leaning back. "Mushroom season is over . . . What are you all going to do?"

No one spoke.

I sat down on the other side of Chulho. "Well . . . ," I began slowly, my eyes circling the others. I wanted for one of them to jump in, but no one was volunteering. I took a deep breath. "Well, I guess, even though we don't have any blood relationship, we're brothers and family now . . ."

Chulho tilted his head to the side to get a better look at me and then cocked an eyebrow. "Go on," he said.

"I guess . . . as brothers . . . we have to protect and trust one another and share everything, even a small piece of bread," I continued, again looking into the eyes of the others to see if any of them, particularly Myeongchul, wanted to take over. "If one of us falls sick, we have to take care of him until he gets better," I said. "If one of us is left alone somewhere, we have to find him. We will never fight against each other. These," I finished, "are the rules."

"So you're a gang?" Chulho said matter-of-factly.

The others all nodded. I breathed a sigh of relief, for I had made up the rules on the spot, hoping everyone would agree.

"Then I'm in," Chulho said, thrusting his fist in front of him and into the middle of the circle we had formed. We all did the same until our knuckles were flush up against one another's. "You need someone like me," Chulho added. "Every gang has to have the wild card. The guy who doesn't care whether he lives or dies."

"As the old Korean proverb says: We all scratch where one itches," Myeongchul said.

We laughed.

Chulho passed the *sool* to Myeongchul, who took a long swig and then passed the bottle to Sangchul. When it got to me, I picked up the bottle and held it to my mouth.

"Drink, drink," Young-bum and Chulho chanted.

I gingerly took a sip. The liquid burned my throat as it went down and made my head feel as if it were on fire. I felt for a moment like I was going to vomit.

Chulho grinned. "The first time is always hard," he said.

"Like watching the first execution," Young-bum had to remind me.

"It gets easier," Chulho said, taking the bottle back.

As the bottle, and then another, made itself around the room that night, that hole inside of me seemed to fill up with something. I began to laugh, feeling carefree, like a butterfly flitting from one flower to another. For a bit, I didn't feel so alone.

My brothers and I drained the last two bottles of *sool* from Young-bum's grandmother's funeral. We saw the sun come up on the tail end of our day. I was staggering, slurring my words, and hugging my new brothers, not wanting to let them go or to surrender to sleep and find that the night had become day again, a gray day in which I burned inside not from *sool* but from knowing that my parents were gone and I was a *kotjebi*, a street boy with no home.

We divided ourselves into two teams. Young-bum, Chulho, Min-gook, and Un-sik would cover the market, meaning they would steal food for us to eat or sell and also steal won. Sangchul, Myeongchul, and I would perform at the train station. Chulho actually volunteered for his group, announcing with a wicked smile that he had no moral issues about thievery and wasn't particularly fond of the arts. "I prefer the art of perfecting me," he said, puffing up his chest.

I walked right up close and stared him down. "There are two rules: We don't steal from children, and we don't steal from old people. Got it?"

Chulho opened his mouth to protest and then caught Young-bum's cold, icy stare. I guess Young-bum wasn't quite as hardened as I had thought.

"Okay, okay," Chulho said, putting his hands up in the air. "You win."

Our plan was to meet back at Young-bum's house, making it our base of operation. I wanted to make sure we lived in the house as much as possible so brokers didn't get it. The others were happy to not have to sleep outside anymore. The other part of our deal was that we shared everything. We pooled our goods and won together at the end of each day.

LIFE UNFOLDED. OR, RATHER, WE EXISTED FOR ALL OF THE fall and part of the winter. I guess we drifted like the snowbanks. We'd arrive back at the house at different times of the day and empty our bags and pockets into a yellow plastic washing bowl that Chulho had stolen from a woman with a baby. He shrugged when I started to lay into him about how we weren't going to steal from children or old people. "She wasn't old," he said. Chulho liked to push boundaries—I had to give him that much.

At first, when we needed to cook, we took turns. After about a week, Unsik took over. He had a knack for adding a pinch of salt in the right place, or a dried green radish somewhere else, to spruce up any dish, including corn rice. As he cooked, he hummed the revolutionary song "Red Flag."

There are a few things about boys being left on their own that I came to discover during those months. One: With no adult around to lecture us, we could pretty much get away with anything. Chulho and, well, all of us, started to chain-smoke. Chulho also got us talking about things we'd like to do with older women. I'd never heard such talk before, so I blushed in the beginning and turned away. But as the alcohol Chulho said we had to have every day to make it through the winter made its way through my veins, I loosened up and listened.

Sool was hard to steal because the merchants hid it in boxes, so we used either the won we earned performing or the won that Young-bum and the market crew stole to buy alcohol. We stole most of our food, from twisted bread sticks to *dububab* to candy. These foods became pretty much our steady diet during the coldest months so that Unsik didn't have to lug water from the river every night to cook.

Chulho was always the last to fall asleep and the hardest to wake in the mornings. We'd be ready to go, and he'd still be snoring, drooling on his mat, and mumbling women's names.

Young-bum, however, had nightmares, screaming into the night, often calling out for his grandmother. One time, he even thought she was standing in the room, watching over us, holding a white magnolia, welcoming him to the spirit world. "I'm going to die! I'm going to die!" he woke up yelling.

I settled him down, eventually convincing him that what he'd had was a *fear* dream. You know, the kind you have in which your worst fears seem like omens of what's to come. But these were just his mind playing tricks on him, I told him. "I have fear dreams several times a day in which I am sure my parents are dead, their executions watched over by some school class in another city. Then I wake up from my daydream or night dream and tell myself: *fear dream*. You had a night fear dream . . . but same thing. Not real. These are in your mind. Now, dreams that are premonitions of things to come, these are from somewhere else . . . not your mind . . . like a voice in your head telling you not to go down a certain alleyway."

I think Young-bum got it. But he still had nightmares.

When Myeongchul got drunk, he became even chattier, quoting Korean proverbs and acting out different characters, keeping us all in stiches.

Min-gook, who was a quiet guy to begin with, became even more so. Occasionally, though, he'd recite sayings from Kim Il-sung. One night, I hit him on the back of the head with the palm of my hand to get him to stop. "I'm just not sure it's relevant now to keep saying stuff like 'I vow to adopt the communist look, revolutionary work methods, and people-oriented work style.'"

I think he got what I was saying, because he stopped.

Sangchul played games, like the food-fantasy game my father had taught me, even with just himself. "I am thinking of candy, sugar-melting-in-my-mouth candy, shaped like flowers . . . from a wedding . . . ," he would say. I told him that I did that, too, and that my favorite was a yellow tulip candy.

Unsik became like our housemother. Young-bum called him

a *jultagi*, a street boy who stole clothes, mostly from people's clotheslines. He made sure we were always dressed warmly. He also swept and kept things as clean as he could. Before the deep-freeze days of winter came, he'd awake early in the morning and trudge his way through the snowbanks to the river, where he collected water in that plastic yellow laundry bowl he'd use to wash whatever dishes needed cleaning.

But no matter how well Unsik looked after the place, one thing about boys living together in a confined space with no adults hollering at them to bathe is that they also stink. And stinky boys don't smell it on themselves or on one another.

Mi Shun came to tell us she was leaving Shang-gi-ryeong in search of a distant relative in another town who she hoped had food. She stepped into the house, plugged her nose, and then immediately left. Shivering outside, she told Young-bum that we didn't need to worry about brokers stealing her mother's place. It reeked of onions, cigarette smoke, stale alcohol, and our foul body odor. She said she'd never visit again unless we found a way to wash our bodies and the house. But even Chulho, who one night when drunk admitted he had a crush on Young-bum's aunt, wasn't that inspired to change. For one, there was no hot water. We'd have to buy extra wood to heat enough water for all of us to have a bath. Chulho would rather stay dirty than spend his extra cash on wood instead of *sool*.

¤ ¤ ¤

ALTHOUGH WE NEVER SAID SO FORMALLY, IT WAS UNDER-
stood that we were no longer celebrating holidays, like the Day of
the Sun or our birthdays. I thought it was just plain economical to
forget, not having to buy any eggs or pork or to skip a day making
money to party. But the truth was that I wanted to forget what my
life had been like before I'd become a *kotjebi*.

So it was just a few weeks after the winter solstice, when those
short days were dark to begin with, when Young-bum and I figured we actually were bringing home less than was usual, even
taking into consideration that most of the merchants who lived
outside Gyeong-seong, like the fish sellers, were no longer coming to the market and there was little produce left to sell.

"We should still have more," I said.

"I think someone is stealing," Young-bum said out loud what I
was thinking. "I think it's Chulho," he added. "He disappears every
day without telling me where he's going."

I said nothing. But I was playing Chulho's own words over and
over again in my head: *Every gang needs a wild card.* My gut said it
was him, too.

"Why don't you skip performing for a few days and spy on
him?" Young-bum suggested.

I nodded. I had to catch a thief.

WHEN I AWOKE AT DAWN, I DIDN'T GET UP. I MOANED AND
pulled my dirty wool blanket over my face. When I heard the foot-

steps and the voices of the others fade down the road, I slipped out from underneath my covers and ran through the fields until I reached the market.

As soon as I entered, I grabbed a wide-rimmed hat off an old beggar man, promising to give it back. I then trailed Chulho, biting my lip to stop myself from laughing as I watched him flirt with the female vendors. What the women couldn't see, but I could, was a hungover Chulho, standing on wobbly legs, sneaking a hand onto a table and grabbing whatever items were on display that he could hold. As the women batted their eyelashes and stuck their hips out toward Chulho, giggling and blushing from his attention, he'd stuff the items into his bag.

Nothing so far seemed out of sorts.

Until midday.

With that Chulho swagger of his, he grabbed some fried tofu off a tray a woman was carrying and sauntered right out of the market. I followed at a distance, ducking in behind the corners of buildings whenever he looked back. He walked clear through town until he stopped in front of a house with boarded-up windows. He knocked three times and waited. The door swung open and he stepped inside.

I had to see for myself what was going on, so I sneaked up to the building and found a small hole between the boards on one of the windows.

At first, the lighting inside was so dim I saw nothing but the shadows of moving people. Then, as my eyes adjusted, I saw tiny candles set in jars on the floor. A woman sashayed in front of me and I leaped back in shock. But she didn't notice me. I looked in the window again. The woman was about my mother's age, wearing dark gray slacks and an oversize black wool sweater that had a big tear in the back. Her arms and hands moved like birds' wings. She flitted around like a swallow. She eventually sat down in front of another woman, who began to pick lice out of her hair.

Then I heard Chulho talking to another woman, who had an older, crinkly voice, like leaves being rubbed together. I couldn't see him, and I strained to hear the conversation as if it were taking place in another room.

A woman stepped toward the front door to leave. I ducked down behind a garbage bin so she couldn't see me. As she opened the door, a gust of wind scented with some heavy perfume, a body oil maybe, moved out and hit me.

All I could think as I watched her move down the street was how different a house full of girls was from our house full of boys.

I SKULKED BACK TO THE TRAIN STATION, MY INSIDES FEELing like sour milk with a lemon squirted over the top. I was angry. I was hurt. Most of all, I was confused. Someone was stealing from us. Chulho was up to something. A knot in my stomach curled its way up, strangling my throat.

But it was not Chulho who was stealing. That night and the

nights that followed, everything I watched him steal he plopped down in that plastic yellow laundry basket. In fact, he was stealing more food for us than anyone else.

Finally, after following Chulho several times to the women's house, I told Young-bum, "He's not stealing, but he's doing something . . . Something's not right, I can feel it," I said.

"Whatever it is, he'll come clean about it one of these days. You know him," Young-bum said with a sigh. "Chulho's always talking to someone, digging up some piece of information."

Young-bum was right. I had to give it to Chulho; we knew more about what was going on in Joseon through him than through anyone else.

"We still have a thief among us," Young-bum continued.

So I ditched following Chulho and started trailing Unsik. And sure enough, he was the one. He pilfered some fresh buns from the lady who on my first day in the market had told me I was *kot-jebi*. Unsik never turned them in.

After a few days of watching him steal stuff he never brought home, I decided to confront him.

I followed him as he sidled out of the market with a handful of twisted bread, not stopping until he reached a low bridge on the far side of the train station. As some barefooted children looked on with hungry eyes, Unsik ate bread stick after bread stick. I stepped out from the shadows as he was licking his fingers clean.

"I'm sorry," he said in a quivering voice as I gripped him tight around the throat. Urine started seeping through his pants. "I just . . . I was so hungry," he choked out.

"We have a pact!" I yelled. I punched him hard in the face. He fell to the ground, spitting up blood. He then stared up at me with desperate, frightened eyes.

I heard a familiar voice call my name and then the sound of feet running up behind me. "Stop," Chulho said.

I didn't care. All I saw in front of me was a thief.

I was on fire. A fury burned inside me, making me perspire despite the cold weather. I ripped off my shirt to cool down, and then I lunged toward Unsik to kick him.

Hands grabbed my arms and pulled me back before I could. "If we fight against each other, we weaken our link," Chulho hissed right into my ear.

I quickly spun around, raised my fist to punch Chulho, ready to kill him if I had to because he, too, was doing something wrong, and then stopped.

It wasn't Chulho at all, but Young-bum. He looked tired and worn, like the tattered bike tire some of the children now held. They were staring wide-eyed at me. One little girl in a dirty dress with sunflowers on it had a slim, open wound on her cheek, as if a knife had been swiped at her face.

My entire body trembled. "We made a pact," Young-bum continued. "We would never fight against each other, no matter what."

Young-bum let go of me and helped Unsik up.

"I know what I did was wrong," Unsik said, stepping in close, tears streaming down his face. "I won't do it ever again. Can we start over?"

I said nothing.

"Being on our own makes me think strange things sometimes . . . not be myself," Young-bum said in a quiet voice. "Did you know I even wondered . . . when we had nothing to eat for several days in a row . . . I wondered what it would be like to eat a dead person?"

Young-bum started to cry now, too.

I just stared out into nothing.

What I didn't tell him was that I had actually wondered this as well.

ON HIS WAY BACK TO THE HOUSE, CHULHO HAD BOUGHT two bottles of *sool* with won that Sangchul had earned singing. When Chulho walked in through the front door, he raised the bottles high over his head and announced we needed a pick-me-up.

As we drank, we were eerily silent, as if the thick cloud that hung over us had swallowed our voices. At one point, Chulho came clean. He told us that he was having meetings with an old woman who wanted us to sell nightflowers for her. "You know— women, to men, for sex," he said to me. Finally, I got my definition of *nightflower*: a prostitute. "It's illegal to sell and buy sex, and, well, I'm not sure how I feel about it. That's why I didn't tell you. The old woman wants us to go to the train station and find men for the women and bring them back," Chulho explained. "But the more I talked to her, the more I came to understand that the women she was selling were just poor, hungry mothers trying to feed their kids.

"So I get it now," he continued, looking at me. "These women could be our own mothers somewhere."

"Even you have a moral compass?" Young-bum said with a grin, punching him playfully on the shoulder.

Any other night I would have laughed, thinking that Chulho actually had a human side. But not this evening.

We all fell silent again. I was angry at Unsik, at Chulho for taking so long to tell us about these meetings, and also at myself for reacting the way I did. I could have killed Unsik, that much I knew for a fact. Wind trickled in through the gaps between the window and the wall. I felt it calling me, so I decided to sleep outside.

I made my way with my blankets to a clearing near the river. I wanted to be alone. But as I sat down on a large, dry rock and wrapped the blankets around me, I heard the sound of approaching feet. I turned to see that the others had all followed me.

"Can we join you?" Young-bum asked in a timid voice.

"Why not?" I snapped. "As long as you're quiet. I want to sleep."

I lay down on my back, my hands behind my head. I strained to find the biggest and brightest star, which was low in the winter sky. When some clouds finally moved and Ursa Major came into view, my mind drifted back to Pyongyang. My anger lifted a bit, and in its place was a burning sadness.

"When I was a little kid, I wanted to be a general in the army," I said out loud. "That dream seems now like it belonged to a different life, one that I never really lived."

After a long silence, Young-bum said, "I wanted to be a truck driver, so I could visit all the cities and get rich."

"I wanted to be a singer for our great leader, Kim Il-sung," Sangchul said.

"I wanted to be a professional marathon runner and advertise my country to the world," Min-gook said next.

"You may not believe this," Chulho began, "but I wanted to be a party leader. A big party leader. Head of the party for Gyeong-seong."

I stifled a laugh. Oddly enough, I could see Chulho as a party leader.

"My dream was to become an actor, in case you didn't know," Myeongchul said. We all jumped on him. Of course we knew. "Stop," he eventually called out. "I'm serious. I wanted to be the next Gil-nam Lee, the action hero in the movie *Order 027*. The next big Joseon action hero. I still do and will be," he said. "Failure is the mother of success, after all."

I rolled my eyes.

"Stick to radio, since you're not that handsome," Unsik chimed in. "Even I'm a better-looking guy, and that's not saying much."

The latter was kind of true. Unsik had a big nose and a round face. Myeongchul had a nose that was flat. His face was long, like a green pepper, and his eyes were small, staring out into the world like the black buttons on my father's winter coat.

"What did you want to be?" I asked Unsik.

"I don't know," he said wistfully after a long pause, his voice suddenly sad. "I liked math, I guess. But I . . . you know . . . I knew I'd finish high school, join the army, serve my mandatory time there, then go and work where the government sent me. I didn't really have any dreams. Just things like math and doing experiments in the science lab."

"I liked math, too," I said in a quiet voice. "Maybe we have more in common than we think."

"I miss my parents," he then said.

The cloud swallowed us again.

I kept staring at the brightest star, viewing it not so much on this night as a beacon, something I wanted to believe would lead me out of this dark tunnel, but instead as a place I'd rather be. As my teeth started to chatter and my body shook from the cold, I decided to go back into the house. "Anywhere but here," I whispered as I got up to leave. "I wish we had been born anywhere but here."

THAT NIGHT I DREAMED OF PYONGYANG.

I entered the front gates of Mangyeongdae Yuheejang. I reached out to the sides as if I were a star and grabbed my parents' hands: eomeoni's to the right, abeoji's to the left. "High," I shouted. "Swing me high." And they did.

I heard the laughter of children on the roller coaster as it swooped down and around me.

Abeoji, with a wide smile, handed me a small paper bag of stale bread. I called out to the swans on the Daedong River. A black swan with bloodred eyes skirted closer than the white swans I wanted to feed and ate the bread, catching the pieces in the air before they even landed in the water.

Then I wasn't at the amusement park anymore. It was winter. I was panting from sledding. My cheeks were red and chapped from the biting wind; my hands and feet numb from the cold. Eomeoni tore off my mittens and wrapped my frozen fingers in hers.

"I made rice cookies," she whispered.

In my dream, I was back in my apartment in Pyongyang, which was filled with the aroma of sesame.

17

W e need to move," Young-bum said. It was midwinter 1999, nearly a year after my father had left for China. I thought we needed to leave Gyeong-seong, too, but had not brought it up with Young-bum or any of the others. If we left, Young-bum would lose his house. Brokers would take it—that was almost a certainty. I wanted the decision to leave to come from Young-bum and from him alone.

But the truth was, we were struggling.

Kotjebi from all over the country had flocked to Gyeong-seong, like migrating geese. But unlike migrating birds that traveled to warmer climates in the winter, including as far away as New Zealand, the *kotjebi*'s internal radar was slightly off. These hungry boys thought Gyeong-seong was the answer, not realizing we likely had even less than they had where they came from. Now we were all competing for very limited resources, and the newer the *kotjebi,* the better they seemed to do. Mostly it was because the merchants knew who we were, all of us. When they saw any of us come into the market, they would hide their goods. It was getting harder and harder for us to steal, so we had to rely more and more on the money we made performing.

The problem with this was that Myeongchul was running out of ideas for plays he could put on. Sure, there was no shortage of stories to choose from: Kim Il-sung's childhood tests showcasing his physical and emotional strength; his love and devotion to his mother, Kang Ban-sok; and his overthrow of the Japanese colonialists. Myeongchul, however, had been at the train station for more than a year now. He had to repeat skits, and his audiences were getting bored, drifting over to watch the new *kotjebi.*

Trying to keep the spectators' interests alive, Unsik, Sangchul, and I wrote some original material. In one skit, Myeongchul plays the hero who saves the audience from villains, which were played by Unsik and me. Myeongchul was like Boy General, swooping in on his horse, a long stick, flailing his sword, also a long stick. The play started when Unsik whistled, because he could whistle louder than any train to get people's attention. And we had that. For about a week. Then the audience moved downstream to watch the newer talent.

The *kotjebi* gangs streaming into the market, some coming from as far away as Hamhung, were so desperate for food that they would fight anyone for it. Young-bum was strong. He could look after himself when he faced foes. And Unsik and Min-gook were fast. They could escape easy enough when another *kotjebi* pulled out a chain or a broken bottle. But Chulho had a lot of puffed-up bravado inside him. He instigated a lot of fights, and he was always nursing a sliced-open side or a knife wound on his hand as a result.

"If we don't move, Chulho's going to get killed," said Young-bum, as if telling me something I didn't know. "Let's head north, spend a few weeks in a town or city before moving on to another," he suggested.

I nodded. The others agreed, too.

We'd start in Cheongjin, the provincial capital of Hamgyeong-bukdo, the third-biggest city in Joseon. Our plan was to stow away on one of the coal trains just as it was leaving the Shang-gi-ryeong station.

We all helped Young-bum nail planks of wood across the doors and windows of his house, in the hopes that if we made the place look as if it were falling down, it might keep the brokers away while we were gone. I wasn't optimistic it would work, but it was worth a try.

When night fell, we ate *dububab*. Young-bum was quiet as he chugged a bottle of *sool* on his own and looked around his house for the last time.

"We'll be back," I tried to reassure him.

As I said this, I made a vow to myself that when we returned to

Gyeong-seong, I would reclaim not only Young-bum's house but also my own house and then clean it for my mother.

BOARDING THE COAL TRAIN WAS NOT AS HARD AS I'D EXpected. It was a new moon, for one, and a cloudy night. So it was dark, almost pitch-black. There was also no wind and, well, little noise other than my racing heartbeat and the sound of us boys breathing. For some reason, that kind of scared me, that and there being so few people milling about, including *kotjebi*. It was a night like the one when I arrived in Shang-gi-ryeong. If I hadn't been with my brothers, I might have been a bit scared of *yu-ryeong*.

We climbed up the ladder and then hid under the coal.

I only looked up when I felt the train reach its full speed. Then I sat up, spread my arms out to the side as if I were a bird, and exhaled. We were moving through the mountains, north, where the air was even fresher than in Gyeong-seong.

WE ARRIVED IN RANAM STATION ON THE OUTSKIRTS OF Cheongjin looking as black as the night, our skin, hair, and clothes covered in coal dust. Our hair was so matted with the stuff that Unsik suggested we steal a pair of scissors, cut off all our hair, and then use Young-bum's razor to shave the rest. We, indeed, looked as if we'd just been dug out of graves, but I thought of the people I'd seen at the train stations on my way to Gyeong-seong from Pyongyang: the old people and children with frizzy hair and bald patches. I told Unsik I'd rather walk around looking like death itself than cut my hair. "I'm still alive and healthy," I told him. "So until I get sick and lose my hair without the use of any scissors, I'd like to keep what I have." I vowed then and there that if I ever got the opportunity to live in a house again where there was a bath, I would never be dirty again.

The Ranam train station was full of men, some unloading the train, others milling about drinking *sool*. I guessed that the latter were too out of it to really notice us. Or maybe they'd seen kids like us before and didn't care anymore. Either way, no one seemed to notice when we climbed down off the coal train and slunk through the station, looking for the exit.

We headed into town and in the direction, I hoped, of the coast, where, despite the cold weather, if we reached the water, I was going for a swim.

WE WALKED AND WALKED, MEETING NO ONE UNTIL SHORTLY after dawn, when we came upon two old women pushing a cart of dried mackerel. Cheongjin, the women with sea-wrinkled faces told Chulho, had four open-air markets: Ranam, Pohwang, Sunam, and Songpyeong. "Ranam Market is just around the corner," one of the women said, grabbing my arm and pulling me down the street, leaving the boys and the other woman to push the cart. When we turned the corner, my breath was knocked out of me. The market stretched out before me for as far as I could see.

There were so many people, even at this early hour, it could have been Parade Day in Pyongyang.

"Let's explore," Chulho said, catching up to me and then taking off.

I waded into the market behind him, trying not to get distracted by the colors and smells, studying which vendors sold what foods and, more important, locating the *kotjebi* gangs that my brothers and I needed to avoid.

For more than eight hours I meandered through the market, stealing candies and twisted bread. Chulho and Young-bum, using the double-razor-brick trick, got a few purses, too.

As the sun finally began to set, streaking the sky in pale pink ribbons, the boys and I met up again where we first entered the market. We needed to find somewhere to sleep that was warm. We were heading down the road, back in the direction of the train station, when we ran right into another *kotjebi* gang: boys older than us, dirtier, more confident and more sure-footed. I could tell that just by the way they stood facing us.

"Who are you?" the tallest of the boys asked, stepping toward us.

My brothers and I looked at one another and shrugged. None of us knew who should speak.

"Where are you from?" the boy demanded, clenching his fists, preparing for a fight. Some of his crew grasped wooden poles in their hands. The sight of these made me shiver.

"Gyeong-seong," I finally replied nervously, my eyes darting from one boy to the other. If we had to fight them, we had one thing going for us: There were six of them and seven of us.

The boy spat, his saliva landing on my shoe. "Leave," he said with a snarl. "There is no room for you here."

I shook my head slowly. "We can't leave," I said.

"You have two choices: Leave or fight," the boy said, walking toward me. He stopped so close I could feel his breath, hot and sticky, on my cheek.

"Fight," I said nervously. I wished Chulho had taken over talking or that Myeongchul had come up with some Korean saying that would make us all laugh and we'd become friends.

The boy scowled. "Are you sure you want to fight?" he asked. "Have you ever done this before?"

"Of course," I said. What was there to know? His gang would fight my gang.

"Well, then, you know that in street fighting, the leaders of the groups usually fight against each other. It's kind of the rule of the *kotjebi*. If we all fought and we all got injured, then, well, no one would be left. So we fight one-on-one."

I grunted, "Uh-huh," as if I already knew this. But I didn't. Back in Gyeong-seong, *kotjebi* gangs fought each other informally. These Ranam boys, though, had rules for *kotjebi* fighting that I had no clue about. My mind churned with who was going to be our leader. We had never discussed this. And while I was confident of our fighting as a group, one-on-one was different. Individually, none of us was strong enough.

I felt as though I was going to vomit and pass out, not certain which would come first.

"So, who is your leader?" the boy asked. He had a slim mustache and narrow, beady eyes. An old scar cut his chin in half. He must have been sixteen or seventeen, I figured.

"Who is your leader?" he repeated in a raised voice. I opened my mouth to say Chulho when I heard the sound of feet shuffling behind me. I turned. My brothers had all taken a step back, leaving me to face the boy.

My mouth was dry all of a sudden.

"So *you're* the leader!" The boy smirked. He started pounding his fist into the palm of his hand. "Glad that's finally settled."

As I took a deep breath to calm my nerves, the boy pounced, knocking me to the ground and the wind out of me. The entire weight of his body fell hard on top of me, pinning me. Instead of getting off then, as in tae kwon do, he clung hard, so close and tight I couldn't use any of my tae kwon do skills to fight back. I couldn't even push him away to get out from under him to punch and kick. It was as if I were inside the jaws of a big whale, and he was clamping down hard, choking me around the neck with one hand and punching my face with the other.

This boy wasn't made of blood and bones but the wind of fury. This boy could kill me unless I surrendered.

Finally, the boy pulled himself off me. I rolled over onto my stomach, gasping for air, my lip swelling, my entire body bruised and bloodied and tingling from the trauma.

"You have two choices," he said, kicking me hard in the ribs one more time. "Leave, or join us and work under us."

y brothers and I trudged our way back to the train station, like mourners, carrying the embarrassment of having been defeated in battle and being forced to leave the market. None of us had any intention of remaining and working under another gang.

In a corner of the waiting room, my brothers had me lie down. Unsik got some clean water from a woman selling tofu soup. Chulho tore off the bottom of his shirt, which Young-bum ripped into several strips to use as bandages. As they looked after me, I drifted in and out of sleep. When I was awake, I'd see my brothers' eyes peering down at me, big, black, and glossy, the way fish looked when laid out on trays at the market.

Young-bum had me sit up at one point and fed me some bread. He also gave me an egg. As he did, I felt a tightening in my chest, for I remembered my mother then. When I was four, I had fallen off the slide at the day-care center. "*Adeul*," she had said, handing me an egg. "Roll this over your sore arm, back and forth, like I use a rolling pin in the kitchen. The egg will take the swelling down."

I bit my lip to stop myself from crying. I really hated it when these memories hit me like this. I felt pulled under by a huge ocean wave.

I hurt all over.

I missed *eomeoni*.

AS THE PALE LIGHT OF MORNING STREAMED THROUGH THE station windows, I finally fully emerged from my dream state. Young-bum, who was lying beside me, was just opening his eyes, too.

"I know what you're going to say," he said, propping himself up by the elbow.

"What?" I said, turning my face away from him, in part because he stank, with his morning breath and bad body odor, and also I felt sick again. I didn't want to vomit on him.

"You're going to tell the others that you're stepping down as our leader. But don't," he said, turning my head so I had to look at *and* smell him. "From this day on, you are our leader, our *daejang*."

"But I lost the fight," I said, moaning from both the shooting pain that ricocheted through my body and the pain of my bruised ego.

"Yes, but you led our student council. You are brave and smart and courageous. We trust you."

I looked at my brothers, who were now all awake, some rubbing their eyes filled with gunk. "I'm not your leader," I whispered to them. "I'm not strong enough."

"We trust you," Sangchul and Unsik said at the same time.

"I may act brave, but I would have run away," Chulho added, lighting up a cigarette.

I scrunched up my face as he did so. "You're not even up yet and you're smoking!" I exclaimed.

He rolled his eyes.

"You brought us all together," Myeongchul continued. "You always scratch where it itches."

I wanted to make a joke about Myeongchul's proverb, but it hurt too much to laugh.

"We would all be dead right now if it wasn't for you," Mingook said instead.

I wasn't sure that was true, but I agreed to act as their leader, at least for a little while.

I STOOD UP TO STRETCH MY LEGS, WHICH ALSO HURT. I looked around for my running shoes, a black pair I had brought with me from Pyongyang. But they were nowhere. On the floor beside me, where I thought I had placed my shoes the night before, was a pair of thin sneakers with the soles falling apart. I scratched my head and scanned the train station. My eyes landed on a young *kotjebi* near one of the exits who was staring at me. When I caught his eye, he bowed to say thank you.

"Did you steal my shoes?" I called out, my voice echoing against the concrete walls. "Did you take mine and replace them with these?" I held up the tattered sneakers for him to see.

"In future, you should tie your shoes around your neck when you sleep!" he yelled back. He then left quickly, too quickly for my brothers and me to chase him down.

Angry, I threw one of the sneakers across the train station floor.

I was still filthy from traveling in the coal train. I was dirty from the fight the day before. My skin was covered in dried blood, bruises, and mud, and was scratched from the tiny stones on the ground on which I had been pinned. My head itched, likely from lice. And now all that I had to wear on my feet were old, broken sneakers.

Chulho and Young-bum each grabbed one of my arms and spun me around as Min-gook slipped his shoes onto my feet. "I'll go barefoot," he said. "I've always wanted to run a marathon barefoot," he added as I opened my mouth to protest taking his shoes.

"This is what I want you to do," Chulho explained as he came in close to me. "I'm going to leap into an open cargo hold as the train is starting to leave the station. I'll get in first to help you up, but you follow me and do the same."

Before I could ask any questions, Chulho took off, with all of us trailing him, me at the very back.

I huffed and snorted like a wounded wild boar.

My ribs hurt, and breathing was difficult. When Chulho rounded the caboose, I lost track of him for a moment. Then he came into view again. He was racing, running even faster than Min-gook, down the tracks on which a train was slowly moving out. Then suddenly he was flying through the air, leaping like a mountain tiger. He disappeared into the cargo hold.

Chulho reemerged to help Young-bum up next. Min-gook flew in, much like Chulho and without needing assistance. Myeongchul raced along the side, his hand outstretched waiting for someone to catch it. Finally, Chulho, with a cigarette dangling from the corner of his mouth, pulled him in. Sangchul and Unsik were each pulled up by Young-bum.

Soon it was just me left. I pushed my legs to move faster as the train started to speed up.

When I neared the open door, I lifted my arms into the air the way I did as a child when I wanted my mother and father to swing me high at the amusement park.

I don't know who grabbed my hand, but whoever it was, he was perspiring. I thought I was going to slip out from his grasp and fall under the moving train.

I felt myself being lifted and my legs leaving the ground.

I screamed as I felt the grip loosen.

But then I saw Young-bum. He held on tight to my lower arm and yanked me into the open cargo hold.

I fell clear across to the other side and landed against the metal wall with a thud.

WE GOT OFF ALMOST AT THE CENTER OF THE CITY AT Songpyeong train station.

We had barely set foot inside Songpyeong Market when we found ourselves cornered by another *kotjebi* gang. I was angry mostly because we hadn't even had time to get food, *sool*, or a pack of cigarettes. Chulho had smoked the last one on the train.

This time, I didn't even try to remain standing when their leader hurled his entire weight down on top of me. As his fists pounded my face, somehow I managed to indicate to him that he had won. As he got off me, he spat in my face and said: "Work under us or leave."

"We'll leave," I said as Young-bum pulled me up.

We hopped another train and got off at Sunam Market. I lost there, too, this time to a boy about half my size. Well, not really. It just seemed that way because he was short, not much taller than Myeongchul. But this guy had a surefire trick: He got me in a hold like a sumo wrestler, with one arm around my leg, the other around my shoulders, and he kicked so hard at my chest with his sharp, pointy knees that I nearly vomited. He also liked to bite. Besides bruises all over my body and too-many-to-count head wounds, I had this scrawny guy's teeth marks on my arms and legs.

WE ARRIVED AT POHWANG MARKET STARVED AND ALL OF us wigging out for cigarettes and alcohol. We waded into the sea of merchants, determined to steal food and buy some *sool* before meeting up with a *kotjebi* gang and my getting the senses knocked out of me.

But, man, what was it with Pohwang? It was as if the *kotjebi* could smell new blood.

As I reached for a twisted bread, the leader of the gang that ruled that section of the market, a tall wiry guy with a long neck, tapped me on the shoulder and flicked his head, indicating "Let's go." I groaned, grabbed the bread stick anyway, and tossed it to Young-bum. Someone should at least eat. I then motioned for the rest of my gang to follow.

The guy led me to an open field that was covered in broken glass. His crew soon formed around him. He stepped toward me and, speaking with a lisp, said: "The loser will leave."

As if I didn't know the rules already.

From my other fights, if you could call them that, I had learned a few things. First off, go in first and fast, grab hold of your opponent, and don't let go. Wrestle him to the ground. Now, since my training was tae kwon do, I had to be able to step back far enough to inflict my kicks and punches. My strategy, if I ever could implement it, was that when my opponent was on his knees or swerving, unlike the others, who just kept hanging on to me, I would let go, move back, and do my tae kwon do patterns.

"Go," one of his sidekicks said.

The tall skinny guy with the lisp lunged toward me fast. But this time it was as if I were watching in slow motion. As he moved, I shot my right leg up and out, my foot landing hard on his groin, forcing him to stumble backward, squealing in pain. I sprang toward him, kicking him hard in the stomach. He fell down on his knees, gasping for air. As I raised my fist to strike his back and face, he lifted a shaky right hand and called out for me to stop.

"You win," he said, wincing.

I stepped toward the boy and offered him my hand. "Leave or come under us," I said.

"We cannot leave here," he said, in between catching his breath. "We will stay and work for you."

THE BOY'S NAME WAS HYEKCHUL, AND HE AND HIS GANG were familiar with Pohwang Market, as they'd grown up nearby. He and his gang were a lot like us, with parents who had either died or left to find food and never came back. They were *pajang-jebi*, Hyekchul explained, whose modus operandi was to knock over a vendor's stand and then steal the items as the merchant scrambled to pick things up.

Hyekchul said that in his first fight with an opposing gang, his upper lip had been cut with a knife so badly that he no longer could speak properly. "The other *kotjebi* make fun of us," he said, "because *pajang-jebi* is considered one of the lowest forms of stealing. Begging is worse," he explained. "But we come right after that."

"The other gangs say we're like ants on their sticky buns," one of Hyekchul's underlings joined in. "They call us weak. They say we shame them. But the truth is, none of us wants to fight. We're just kids wanting to eat—mostly wanting our parents to come home."

I got that, I told him. We were all pretty average kids, too, some of us with big dreams at one time. To be honest, I wasn't sure whether we still had them. Some unspoken rules about street living include never speaking about family or our hopes.

WE STAYED AT POHWANG MARKET FOR SEVERAL WEEKS, sleeping in an old warehouse alongside Hyekchul and his gang. It was dangerous in Pohwang, with the *Shangmoo* and police always looking for boys. Because of this, we took shifts, two of us awake at all times, acting as watchmen.

On the outskirts of the city, I found us all a second home, an old farm shed. It was cold in the shed. For when it was just too risky to sleep in the warehouse and we found ourselves in the shed on blistery winter nights, Chulho and Unsik came up with the idea of making pants and sweaters out of vinyl sheeting that we'd wear like shells, to keep in our body warmth.

Death was all around us. We'd enter the market in the mornings to find women wailing and rocking in their arms children who had died during the night. As we plunged deep into the merchants' stalls, we found the corpses of old men and women, mouths still agape as if, in their final moments, they wanted to say something, their eyes staring out, pleading with us to hear them. I always thought the place after death was peaceful. It was how my *eomeoni* had described it. But what I saw on the faces of the dead was anything but. It was as if they had got stuck looking at and feeling all their grief and pain.

I started to smoke heavily in Pohwang, so much so that I'd awake with a wet cough and my chest feeling tight and on fire.

I bought raw opium from a merchant Chulho got to know. Back at our home base, my gang and I heated the latex from the opium pod on a spoon, mixed the syrup in water, and drank it. The concoction would settle my stomach when I ate a bug or rotten food—at least, that was my excuse. On those days when I did opium, I'd float through the markets, drifting in unknown places in my mind, many of which I can't recall now, but they sure felt like they were nice.

Chulho told me that there was another drug, called ice or *ping-du*, that he'd heard some *kotjebi* gangs used that took them to heaven. This drug, he boasted, helped them forget their hunger. Ice made them confident and gave them more energy to steal and fight.

Chulho looked for it for us, but he couldn't find it.

I eventually chalked the mystery ice drug up to folklore, which Myeongchul explained was make-believe stories that helped people cope with difficult lives. "It's like if we believe the drug exists, then we'll keep going until we find it. In moments of despair, we'll pick ourselves up because we want to find this thing that people say takes us to heaven," he said one night right around my thirteenth birthday, a birthday I wanted to forget. I hadn't told the others, but that day I had sipped my opium drink from noon until nightfall. It was my way of celebrating, I guess.

"Uh-huh," I said, thinking instead of the *Learning Journey of a Thousand Miles*. "It's kind of a folk story, too?" I asked Myeongchul, who nodded. I was so high that, for a brief moment, I felt as if I were Kim Il-sung stuck up in those mountains.

"It's a folk story, a good one," he replied matter-of-factly. "Folklore has a funny way of becoming truth. If we didn't have folk stories, we might start to question our lives, our governments, our world . . . We might start . . . thinking for ourselves."

"Ah," I said, floating on the ship of opium. I don't think he noticed.

"Right now," he leaned in close and whispered conspiratorially, "we're in the middle of a river, with one bank being our old lives filled with those folk stories that helped control us and which made us feel safe. The other bank, the one we are trying to swim toward, is the unknown."

"Ah," I said again, thinking to myself that I didn't mind the middle part of this journey so much as long as I had opium to calm the waters.

UNSIK, WITH HIS DISTINCTIVE WHISTLE, CLIMBED A TALL post in the market and perched himself at the top. His job was to whistle—"one long"—to let us know if the *Shangmoo* had caught our scent. Two short whistles meant the police were following us.

One day, as the azaleas were just starting to bloom, the *Shangmoo* not only hunted Min-gook and me down as we meandered through the stalls, two policemen joined in as well, forcing us to split up. We started heading toward the abandoned farm shed, but instead we ducked behind a building and let them pass. The *Shangmoo* and the police went right to our safe house. I stole through the back alleys to a large boulder about a block from the safe house, which we had all agreed would be our marker. I took three pebbles, just as my father had taught me when we played toy soldier in Pyongyang, and laid them at the foot of the boulder to tell my brothers and Hyekchul's band not to go to the shed. What was once a game had now become real. I had taught the others how to use small stones to communicate with one another. What I was saying on this day was that we'd been busted.

That night, Hyekchul's gang and mine split up. We let his gang take the shed.

My brothers and I headed to the forest.

IT WAS A NOISY NIGHT AND RAW, THE COLD GETTING RIGHT inside our bones so much that even the vinyl sheeting couldn't keep the chill at bay. We all stayed awake, shivering, huddled together, waiting for morning and the chance to slip back into the train station to get warm. We were all quiet, including, uncharacteristically, Myeongchul. We listened to the wind and the night noises.

"I think we should stop calling each other by our real names," Min-gook eventually said at dawn.

None of us had slept.

"If we have fake names and we're caught, the party can't track down our family members and hurt them," Myeongchul added.

"What should I be called?" I asked, thinking *Boy General* would be most fitting.

I could hear my brothers scratching their chins. Chulho and Unsik were starting to show man-stubble.

"Chang," Chulho eventually called out. *Chang* means "spear" in Korean.

"Why?" I exclaimed. "After all, you're more like a Chang. When I first met you, I thought you were the one who was piercing and sharp."

"It's only my mouth that stings," Chulho replied with a sinister laugh. "Inside, I am more like soft tofu."

We all chuckled at that.

"I think 'Chang' is a good name for you," Young-bum said. "You're quieter, for sure, than Chulho and Myeongchul, but when you speak, we trust your words because we know you've thought things through. I know you would die for me. You are direct and sharp like a spear."

"When you fought Hyekchul, you were focused, just like a spear whizzing through the air toward its target," Unsik added. "I saw that same look when you performed your tae kwon do patterns for the first time at the market. It's like something takes over."

"I wish something would take over for me in every fight," I muttered.

I ran the word *Chang* over my tongue. I liked it. "From this day on," I finally announced, "I shall be known as Chang."

The morning that I came to be called Chang, my gang and I discussed moving on because the *Shangmoo* had discovered our hideaway. While we didn't say it to ourselves or to one another, I think we all secretly wished that we'd go back to Gyeong-seong and find our parents home.

"A plan is a plan, and we vowed that we would head north and work our way back to Gyeong-seong," Myeongchul said, waving his fingers in the air as if he were drawing a map. "We're here," he said, pointing. "Let's start making our way back to there."

Hyekchul and his gang weren't ready to leave the area where most of them grew up. Some fortune-tellers had told them tales that the famine had ended. Hyekchul and his posse had paid them a small fortune of their hard-stolen won to do spells to bring their families back together. Hyekchul and his boys still had hope, lots of it, that soon they'd see their mothers and fathers. The fortune-tellers promised them. I was now a full-blown skeptic. But I didn't want to take their hope away from them by making them move with us, so I released their gang.

"You're free to go," I said on the rainy day when we said good-bye. As I spoke, lightning flashed over the southern hills. "I hope we've taught you well so the next gang you meet you'll beat and they'll fight under you, not you under them."

Hyekchul nodded and gave me a long hug, showing affection I wasn't used to from a friend. When he finally pulled away, his eyes were bursting with water like the spring rivers. "I'm scared being without you," he said.

I rubbed his back and told him that it would be okay, that he and his group had skills now and would make it to the other side of the riverbank, the unknown side, where his family was waiting for him. He thought that I was speaking about the Duman River and that his parents were on the other side, in China.

My gang and I hopped the freight train to Rajin-Seonbong, which was an economic zone, Chulho explained, in which Chinese, Russian, and Joseon merchants all sold goods. "We can get things in Rajin-Seonbong that we can't get anywhere else, like fur hats, chocolate made with milk and mint, and this alcohol called vodka that goes down your throat smooth like cream."

Not like *sool*, which always, no matter how much I drank, burned its way through me.

"Maybe in Rajin-Seonbong we can get jobs on a ship," Myeongchul said, his voice wistful and dreamy. "Maybe we can put our lives as *kotjebi* behind us."

I let my mind wander to thoughts of a life sailing the seas.

"I'll wake to the sound of gulls," Myeongchul continued, as if describing my daydream, "and I'll eat mackerel for breakfast and lunch."

The way Myeongchul talked, I could see us all there on some big fishing ship, our faces sun-kissed and our hands calloused from pulling up the fishing nets and separating the crabs from the fish.

"Stop," I eventually said, more to myself than to him. "I don't want to think of such things. Even if we landed jobs, we'd still be *kotjebi*, because in Joseon no one is allowed to work until they're eighteen. We'd be slave laborers. The captain could pay us nothing and starve us to death."

Myeongchul looked at Chulho, who shook his head and pursed his lips before saying, "Sometimes it's nice to daydream. You really can be sour sometimes."

"Really?" I said, glaring at him. "I'd say your nickname is 'Dream Wrecker,' because since I first arrived in Gyeong-seong, that's all you've ever done—get me to look at the facts rather than believe in something better."

Myeongchul sighed. "I don't want to fight. Not now. At least it was a nice dream," he whispered, blushing and lowering his head.

"Dreams are beautiful," I said to him in a soft voice, trying to be more upbeat. "Keep it, because you never know."

"Dreams are one thing the government can't take from us," he replied, looking up.

"Yeah, but they sure try," Chulho complained.

I rolled my eyes at him and pounded my fist into the palm of my hand, indicating "Enough."

MY BROTHERS AND I DECIDED ON THE TRAIN TO RAJIN-Seonbong that we would not wait to be cornered by any *kotjebi* gang. We would search them out and jump them first.

Rajin-Seonbong Market was beside the harbor. A large freight ship, with crates piled high with what Chulho said were English markings, was moored there. I stopped to stare, for the ship was heavily guarded by military. Workers were moving the crates off on trolleys and loading them into a large and heavily guarded truck.

"I bet that's all going to Pyongyang," Young-bum said in a hushed voice, coming up behind me.

A shiver ran through me because I knew he was right.

I led my gang into the market, which was much like all the others: stalls upon stalls, manned mostly by disheveled men, who I suspected had had big government jobs until all went to rot up here, and a few of their wives; people hawking wilting produce, likely taken out of underground freezers where it had been stored since harvest season; and a few professional vendors, who were better dressed and more filled out. What was different was that there were cars driven by Russian and Chinese businessmen, large cars that would push themselves through the crowds of people. None of my brothers except Chulho had ever seen a white person before, so we stopped to stare at the Russian drivers. Both the drivers' and my brothers' expressions were a mix of awe and fear. I slapped Unsik and Young-bum on the back to get them out of their daydream and told them we had business, too, or else we'd starve. "Let's go and get breakfast."

In Rajin-Seonbong Market there was white rice, tofu, seaweed, and fresh fish, some of which was dried and hanging off clothes-pegs on lines stretched behind the vendors. I was looking at these fish, some skinned pink, others fully whole and blue, when suddenly something made me look up. I stopped dead in my tracks.

I snapped my fingers twice, indicating to my gang, who were behind me, to do the same.

I then pointed at this jumpy kid wearing gray slacks with holes in them and a dirty gray jacket. He was skittish as he looked around, not yet noticing me, reminding me of a field weasel. He sniffed the market, looking for something. But what caught my attention was the way the merchants looked at him: as if they were afraid. It could have been my imagination, but I felt the merchants were backing away to give him space to steal whatever he liked.

"I'm sure this boy is part of the gang ruling the market," I whispered to Unsik, who was now standing beside me.

"Or its leader," he shot back. "I don't like the look of him. Shifty. Ruthless, like he'd pull a chain or, worse, a knife."

Easy fight, I thought. "He's thin," I replied. "He's on some drug and lost in some mist of whatever it is that's making his skin yellow and his nerves twitch like sardines frying in soybean oil. Look more closely.

"Hey, you," I called out to the guy in a confident, strong voice. I wanted him to get the message right at the get-go that my gang and I had arrived and were taking over. "Where's your leader?" I shouted, taking a few steps toward him.

He stopped, turned to look at me, squinted his eyes, and puckered up his lips. "Who are you?" he asked in a voice that made me take a step back. It was like a gale, like the voice of the man who had taken over my house back in Gyeong-seong and eventually threw me out the front door.

"This guy has no fear," I whispered out loud. "Chang," I replied. "I lead this gang. Who's the leader in charge of the gang who rules this market?"

"We don't have leaders here," said the boy, who I guessed was about sixteen. His voice was cold and empty, like a week-old corpse. "The alley, in one hour. Be there," he continued, pointing to some buildings on the far side of the market. He took a few steps toward me, then stopped. He was close enough now that I could see his face. He had a crooked mouth and wide, high cheek-bones, pockmarked from some skin disease. He opened his mouth and grinned. His gums were black, and his teeth were yellow, like his skin. The whites of his eyes were yellow, too, and his enlarged pupils moved over us like spotlights, back and forth. Whatever he was on was not opium. Whatever this guy was on made him smell sweet and brought him back to life. I shuddered, thinking that the drug that takes a person to heaven might actually exist after all. And if it did, this boy was on it.

"We call over there the 'cemetery,'" he continued. "Today it will be your funeral."

I wanted to know who "we" were, but before I could get the question out, the boy had spun around and swiped some electronic wire from the merchant who had been standing around listening to us talk.

The merchant didn't even flinch. It was as if he were used to it. It was as if he knew it was better to let this guy take what he wanted than stand up to him.

AS WE MADE OUR WAY THROUGH THE MARKET TOWARD THE alley, I bent down and grabbed handfuls of stones from the ground, which I then wrapped inside T-shirts I swiped off tables and tied as bags to be used as weapons. Chulho picked up a wrench. Young-bum and Unsik knicked wooden poles. It was like we knew this fight would be different.

The alley was cloaked in the shadow of the abandoned buildings that stood on both sides of it. And the way the alley was positioned between these buildings, I could no longer hear the sounds of the market. Instead, there was a wind, as if we were in some kind of tunnel—a wind that seemed to swallow us up. I felt like I was inside a coffin.

I heard a scratching sound and jumped. My heart raced. "It's just rats," Chulho said, putting a warm hand on my shoulder.

Then there was the flapping of wings. I jumped again.

A raven was taking off, with a long piece of raw flesh dangling from its talons.

We turned a corner, and there they were, six of them, all of them like the boy from the market: wild-eyed and jittery, but not like Young-bum at school. These boys were like the alley, like Joseon . . . *hollow and haunted*. The holes inside them had grown so big that only cobwebs, shards of glass, and *yu-ryeong* roamed around within. These boys may have once had families, had dreams, felt love, had hope, but now the bricks and mortar that held them together were whatever drug they were on. That much I could read off them.

"Who is your leader?" I called out, mustering up the strongest, most authoritative voice I could find. It was hard. Every muscle in my body was twitching to turn around and run away.

"*What?*" several boys said at once, looking at one another and then at us.

"I told you, we don't have leaders," the boy I had met at the market spat out.

"We fight together," another said.

My hands grew clammy and my heart started to race. I didn't know what to do or say. I was the only one of my brothers prepared physically and emotionally to fight. My brothers were soft, especially facing a gang with no fear.

I opened my mouth, wanting to make a deal with them to let me fight their strongest and in return we would leave Rajin-Seonbong. But I didn't have the chance. They came at us, waving metal pipes and broken bottles.

Everything became a blur as arms flailed toward and around me. My mind couldn't keep up with my body, so I just stopped thinking and, as my tae kwon do master had taught me, let technique take over. I watched myself, as if seated in an audience high above, dodge weapons being thrust at various parts of my body. I heard that *thump* of a fist pounding on flesh, and I started kicking anything in front of me with a ferociousness I didn't even know was inside me.

Then I saw blood . . . *blood* pouring from my brothers' faces and onto their shirts, so I attacked even harder anyone who was in front of me, in front of my brothers. I started swinging my T-shirts of stones, hearing them crunch against bone. Much later, my brothers would tell me I was like a superhuman, a real-life Boy

General. "You could have conquered Japan on your own," Chulho would say one day with a laugh.

But that conversation would take place much later.

Slowly, one opposing gang member after another retreated until, finally, I was staring into the wild yellow eyes of the boy I had met at the market. He put up his hand to indicate I had won. But I wasn't about to give him any concessions. I went at him, kicking him in the stomach, then the groin, and finally the head, until he stumbled backward, hit his head hard against a concrete wall, and slumped to the ground. I then spat in his face.

"Don't ever come back here," I said as he moaned and fell unconscious. I didn't kill him, that much I knew. But I wanted to.

I bent over, hands on my knees, to catch my breath. All the while, my eyes were closed and my mind was thanking whatever force had allowed us to beat this group of seriously nasty boys. Then something startled me, and I looked up.

It wasn't a noise. It was silence, like the wind being sucked back up, as if I were standing in the eye of a hurricane, as if I were inside that coffin again.

Hair stood up on the back of my neck as if the *yu-ryeong* had found me this time. I turned around.

Chulho, Sangchul, Min-gook, Young-bum, and Unsik were huddled around Myeongchul, who was lying on the ground.

We already know the things that will happen to us in life. We spend our days just waiting for them to be revealed. I heard my grandfather's words as I walked toward them.

Myeongchul had a huge gash on the side of his head. His entire face was plastered in blood.

"He's d-d-dead?" I sputtered as I collapsed onto my knees.

MY BROTHERS AND I FOUND LONG PLANKS OF WOOD THAT we tied together with strips of our clothes to make a stretcher. We then lifted the moaning Myeongchul onto it and carried him along the dirt road toward the countryside.

On the outskirts of the city, beside a field overgrown with weeds, Chulho spied a farmer's shed that, from a distance, looked abandoned.

Inside, we covered Myeongchul's trembling body with the clothes we were wearing.

"I'm cold and hungry," he managed to choke out. I had to put my ear up close to his mouth to hear him. I felt his forehead. He was clammy and cool. Unsik lit the pine tree stick dipped in resin that he carried with him in a plastic bag around his neck. Once the shed was lit, I could see that Myeongchul was pale, nearly white, like the underbelly of a swan.

Young-bum pulled from his bag a stale twisted bread stick, which he started to break into pieces for Myeongchul to suck on.

Myeongchul, however, reached up and waved for Young-bum to stop.

"Don't forget our first rule. We have to share," he whispered into my ear. He then smiled, his teeth white against lips that were turning blue. With shaky hands, he broke the bread stick into seven pieces.

Myeongchul drank some water that Chulho had collected from a nearby stream and then told a few proverbs, his voice becoming stronger as the night wore on, which made me relax a bit, thinking he would be all right once he ate and rested.

I cleaned his wounds, the way my brothers had cleaned mine after I had lost my fights. Then, as Myeongchul's eyes fluttered back and forth into sleep, Sangchul sang the lullaby my mother sang to me as a child.

> *"Hushabye, hushabye baby*
> *sleep well*
> *go to a country of dream*
> *my lovely baby*
> *go to a country of dream*
> *my lovely baby."*

We eventually left Myeongchul alone to sleep while we stood outside and smoked.

As we took long drags on our cigarettes, we talked in hushed voices about how we had won a battle against probably the worst foes we would ever face. Chulho agreed that this gang was likely on the drug that took people to heaven. "*Ping-du*," he told us. "See, that drug is not a folk story!"

"We should stay in Rajin-Seonbong for a while," I said, changing the subject. "I got a feeling those merchants wanted those boys out of there. They might be nice to us."

"Maybe Myeongchul is right, and we might even find real work on the ships here," said Min-gook.

Chulho laughed. "There is no work for kids," he said. "Such is the life of us kings of the nation."

Since chatterbox Myeongchul wasn't there to say anything, we soon fell silent. After we finished two packs of cigarettes among us, we crept back into the shed and fell asleep on some hay.

I dreamed again of Pyongyang that night and of Mangyeongdae Yuheejang, of *abeoji* and *eomeoni* swinging me high into the air. I saw the hill near the Daedong River where I went tobogganing in the winter.

In my dream, though, I started to cry, for in the middle of it, I knew . . . *I knew* . . . I was dreaming. "I'm a street boy," I told myself. Then I heard Myeongchul's voice digging its way toward me.

"A nobody, a lost boy, a dead boy," he said, his voice faint, as if he were very far away.

I saw myself back in Gyeong-seong Market, late at night, the men drunk, taking swipes at me with their rusty chains, their stench hitting me long before they ever could. Then I saw, in my dream, a dead old man left to rot in the snow, holding his hat in one hand, a small toy soldier in the other.

I heard Myeongchul again. "If you keep your mind, you will survive in a tiger's den," he said.

I went somewhere dark after that, where my dreams and Myeongchul's voice no longer reached.

IN THE MORNING, ALL OF US AWOKE MORE OR LESS AT THE same time, chilled and soaked in dew, for someone had left the door open. We patted ourselves dry with Chulho's extra shirt as we hopped from one foot to the other to warm up. Then we looked out the front door at our surroundings of barren fields. In the distance was a low mountain. We weren't far from Baekdu Mountain, Young-bum said, where Kim Jong-il was born. "My father told me once that there is a lake in Baekdu Mountain made from when a meteor hit the earth. A crater that had fallen from the stars, as if to say Joseon was the chosen place."

I wanted to share with Young-bum my mother's Myth of Dangun, but I remembered Myeongchul and wanted to wake him first.

I shook him gently. "Wake up, Myeongchul."

I then shook him harder.

He was stiff and cold like the ground outside.

He had died sometime in the night.

For the longest time my brothers and I huddled around Myeongchul's body.

Myeongchul, I thought to myself, was our voice. I felt, looking at his corpse, that my throat had been torn from me.

We were all so far away in our own thoughts that we jumped when the door to the shed flew open and a tall figure blocked the light.

"What are you doing here?" a deep, commanding voice demanded. Police. *Shangmoo.* I leaped to my feet and held my hands up over my head.

"I s-s-surrender," I said, my voice trembling. "I mean you no harm, but . . ." My throat hurt too much to talk because, while I couldn't cry, I sure wanted to. I pointed to Myeongchul.

The man stepped into the shed to get a better look. As he did so, I could see him clearly. He wasn't wearing a navy-blue police uniform. I didn't smell that smell—you know, *police.*

Instead, he was wearing the outfit of the Worker Peasant Red Guards, a dirty and tattered khaki Mao-collared jacket and matching pants. He smelled of earth and dew. He worked the farms.

At first, his face was taut. I sensed he was more afraid of us than we of him. But as he bent over Myeongchul, his face softened.

"Where are you from?" he asked no one in particular.

"Gyeong-seong," Sangchul whispered, tears dripping down his cheeks. He wiped them away with the back of his hand, smearing dirt across his face.

The man reached over and shut Myeongchul's open eyelids. He then cleared his throat. "At the mountain," he said, pointing across the field. "I will show you where. You can have a funeral."

THE MAN ALLOWED US TO USE HIS PULL-CART TO WHEEL Myeongchul's body. We walked for about an hour, following the man through the muddy fields, until we reached the foot of the mountain. Then my brothers and I hoisted Myeongchul onto our shoulders and carried him up. We wanted to bury him high so that his grave wouldn't be disturbed by dogs sniffing around for some flesh and bones to eat or by other people looking for a spot to bury their loved ones.

That morning, when I had looked at the mountain, it seemed harmless, like a hiccup in the fields. As we ascended it, though, we had to navigate around sharp crags and dead trees jutting out from the rock face, the roots of which twisted around and hung on to the ledges as an old woman's knotted fingers do her cane.

We stopped at a wide ledge and spread out, looking for a shallow pit in which to bury Myeongchul.

Unsik found an indentation in the ground, deep enough to be used as the burial place, and we laid Myeongchul's body in it.

On top of Myeongchul, we laid pine tree boughs.

Young-bum and Unsik both began to cry, big sobs that made them curl over at the waist. I found myself growing jealous of their tears because I wanted to wail, too.

We all bowed three times.

Instead of leaving right after, though, we stood and stared at the grave.

"You really aren't more handsome than me," Unsik finally said. "I just wanted you to know."

"You really could have been the best actor in the country," Sangchul said next.

Chulho nudged my shoulder. "Say something," he whispered.

I rocked back and forth from my heels to my toes and looked up at the sky. "To live on the streets means we have nothing left," I finally said, then stopped. So many thoughts were moving fast inside my mind, I couldn't catch just one.

"Our families—our pasts—feel like they never existed," I began again. "We're little more than animals now. At least that's what the merchants say about us, and the other *kotjebi*, too. The government once called us the kings and queens of the nation . . . Everyone has abandoned us. Everything has been taken away from us, except hope. You taught me that we can only give hope away. No one can take it. And you also taught me that hope is what makes us human. That, and love. It's time to let you go," I ended. "Leave here. Go find your parents and go to a better place, where you can act all the time and become the next Gil-nam Lee."

BACK AT THE SHED, THE FARMER GAVE US SOME RADISH and rice to eat. Then, dragging our feet, we headed back to the train station, as if we were the losers and not the victors of this city.

I didn't care where we went. Neither did the others. We had grumbled that we would take the first train, and wherever that took us was where we would go. Even though we had won the territory in Rajin-Seonbong, none of us wanted to remain there anymore. There were just too many *yu-ryeong*.

A passenger train was the first to arrive. The police and military were no longer standing like barricades on Parade Day, guarding the steps up to the carriages, as they had on my first train ride from Pyongyang to Gyeong-seong. They now waded deep into the crowd, waving their long batons as if they were farmers cutting hay with long, curved knives.

My brothers and I ducked between some of the carriages and bent down low so as not to be seen. When Unsik whistled that it was safe, we quickly climbed, one after the other, into a freight car with an open door.

We weren't alone. There were many people hiding behind boxes, including an old woman with a baby. They whispered to us with sharp Chulho-like tongues to hunch down low and be quiet. I could hardly breathe on the train once it got moving and the door was shut—there were just too many of us and no air.

We hopped off in the middle of the night at Eodaejin, a port town.

We walked, all of us silent, heads down, dragging our feet, weighted, I guess, by the coat of despair that hung on top of us. Our gang of seven was now six. Without Myeongchul's proverbs and stories, the silence was deafening.

Eventually, I caught the scent of fish and sea salt and then heard gulls cawing and the roar of waves crashing against rocks. The others stopped when they reached the shore. I kept right on walking, over the sand and into the waves, too tired and still in shock over Myeongchul's death to notice until it was too late that the water was freezing. I screamed when the cold hit me. I was angry at . . . well, everything, including that I couldn't even clean myself in the waves. I dragged myself out of the water and lay down in the sand. Covering myself with a blanket, I stared up at the sky. I'd never looked at the sky from the sea, over the top of which the stars curved, wrapping themselves around the earth like a baby's cradle or a mother's arms. It seemed so pure up there. For a moment I wondered what my life looked like, what Joseon looked like, from the stars.

UNFORTUNATELY, WHEN WE FINALLY WALKED INTO EODAE-jin's main market, we discovered that *kotjebi* from across the country had invaded it, much as they had done in Gyeong-seong. My brothers and I didn't want to stay and fight. We had nothing in us, so we made our way back to Cheongjin, planning to go back to Pohwang Market and join up again with Hyekchul.

As when we had first arrived in Cheongjin, the train stopped in Ranam. While we waited for another train to take us to Pohwang, a policeman announced that all the trains had shut down, maybe for a few days, because of no electricity. Hungry, we timidly ventured into Ranam Market, hoping to stay on the outskirts, away from the gang whose leader had defeated me in battle.

We were scoffing bread sticks, candy, cigarettes, and *sool*, when suddenly some female merchants ran past us and some male vendors started yelling. A crowd had formed, and soon there was cheering. My brothers and I crept up and peered through the bodies.

Two gangs were fighting, five on five, or at least that's how many I counted. One gang was made up of a group of kids our age or just a little older. The other gang was a group of young men. I couldn't believe it: boys against men, and fighting right between a stall selling old furniture and a stall displaying farm tools.

The kid gang members were small, but they tossed around weapons that looked like two short sticks tied together with a chain. They swooshed these weapons in the air and then around their bodies. Then *flick!* the weapons moved hard and fast, striking the men across their knees, their ankles, even their stomachs. One member of the man-gang stumbled backward with a head wound that swelled to the size of a football and from which blood spewed like a fountain.

"We can't stay here," I whispered to the others, not taking my eyes off the scene in front of me.

Chulho didn't need to be told twice. He was on his way out of the market before I even turned.

We walked to Pohwang, taking back alleys and an entire night to do so.

WE WANTED TO AVOID GANG BATTLES, BUT WE COULDN'T. For nearly a week in Pohwang Market, my gang met up with other *kotjebi* gang members, who egged us on to fight, sometimes me alone against their leader. A few times, though, all of us waged war. We knew we couldn't keep on running from town to town, so we gave in. Unlike the situation in Rajin-Seonbong, these *kotjebi* gangs were not operating only on the fumes of some mythical drug. They still had hope tucked away somewhere inside them, which meant they held something back in battle. Many were also new to the streets. Most lacked experience in tae kwon do and street fighting. Not once did any gang come near hurting us or chasing us away.

After a week of this and no Hyekchul, we decided to check the other markets to see if he was there. As we were walking out of town, we found ourselves surrounded by a man-gang. A tall, giant

Korean with shoulders the width of a cow said he'd been watching us and was impressed with our speed and strength. "But you lack a lot of skills," he said, "skills that if you don't hone, might get you killed."

Like, really? I thought, rolling my eyes. "We already lost a brother," I spat at him. I was readying myself for a fight. Instead, though, he sighed and stood down.

"I thought so," he said in a sad voice. "You're the guys who beat up the crew in Rajin-Seonbong but lost someone in the process?"

I grunted a yes.

"Come with us," he said, turning and starting to walk out of the market. "We'll help you," he added, waving a hand over his gang of five young men. I'd say all were eighteen or nineteen years old.

"How do we know we can trust you?" Chulho said with a snarl, not moving from his spot. "Maybe you're spies for the *Shangmoo*."

"You can't know," the man said, stopping and facing Chulho. "But you either trust us, wait and see, or leave and face a gang with that weapon that will tear your scalp off if you're not watching."

I shivered, for I knew he was right. Besides, it wouldn't be that bad to work under another gang. We would have to steal and earn won for them. But in return, we would be fed.

"What's your name?" I called out.

"I can't tell you," he said, taking a few steps toward me. "See, we're all dodging our military service. If we say our names and you get arrested and tortured, you might spill who we really are."

I sighed and looked at my brothers, who all nodded slowly.

"Okay," I said. "We'll come with you."

The men led us to an abandoned house on the outskirts of town, a one-room home with a kitchen the size of a small cupboard. The house was empty inside except for some plastic buckets the men used as their toilet and to collect water to bathe, piles of clothes and blankets, and cockroaches, lots of them.

"You can call me 'Big Brother,'" the man said.

"Why are you avoiding your military service?" I asked, looking around at the chipped paint and walls that had concrete falling down from the corners. This house was in even worse shape than my home in Gyeong-seong.

"Please, no questions," he said, raising his hands into the air. "I've told you too much already."

"But you'd have food, be party members. You'd be safe." I was unsure how to size this guy up. I was willing to trust him, but at the same time part of me was certainly not believing him. I wanted to tell him about my life in Pyongyang and how rotten it had become since I had left. "Join the army," I wanted to shout at him. "You'll be safe." But I didn't, for the same reason that Big Brother didn't want to tell us his and his gang's real names or their stories. "I just don't understand. Why would you choose to be homeless rather than fight for our country?" I asked instead. I wasn't expecting him to answer.

Big Brother laughed then, the way Young-bum and Chulho had laughed at me when I asked them questions at school.

"Look," he finally said, as if he were the schoolteacher and I was in first grade. "My gang and I don't believe in Joseon, because it lies to us. It says Joseon is a paradise and children its kings and queens. But children are dying from terrible starvation and diseases. Kings and queens don't die like this. The military are thieves," he said. "They don't protect people; they steal. I don't believe in the army, not anymore."

"What's that weapon? You know, the one that can tear the scalp off a person," I asked next.

"It's a nunchaku, a martial arts weapon from China or Japan. Who knows. On the streets, it's deadly," Big Brother explained. "I run away myself when I see it coming out." Big Brother was like a mountain of hard gray rock. If he was scared of something, then everyone else should be, too.

"How are they getting them?" Chulho asked. I could hear something in his voice: curiosity. He wanted to find a way to get them and sell them.

"They're making them," replied Big Brother. "I mean, maybe someone somewhere is importing them from China to sell to the street kids. But mostly what I'm hearing is that the street kids are making them from oak wood they carve and chains they steal at the market."

"Should we make some?" I asked.

"No. Too dangerous. If that weapon ever got taken away and used against you, *whew!* I have a better weapon for you." Big Brother pulled from his backpack a handful of metal chopsticks, so slim that if they were hurled at someone's eye, I could see them slicing right through to the brain.

"We'll teach you how to use these to both annoy *kotjebi* enough so that they leave you alone and, if necessary, really hurt. But I'm a bit of a pacifist," Big Brother added. "Exert only the force that is necessary to help you survive. No more. There has been too much death already."

"We're with you on that one," Sangchul said.

"What's the deal?" I asked, eyeing Big Brother up and down. "Why are you helping us?"

"We need bodies, young bodies like yours, to steal for us in the market. You're quick and can get in and out before anyone knows anything has been stolen."

"You want us to work for you?" Chulho said.

"Yeah. Give us won and food. Maybe fight alongside us if we have to face a gang all together, not one-on-one. In exchange, we'll give you a place to stay and train you."

"Do we have any choice?" I asked.

"Yeah," Big Brother said. "You can go. It's cruel out there. Another one of you will die, I promise you that. But you can go whenever you want."

I pinched my eyes shut as my brothers huddled around me to

discuss what to do. Big Brother, I knew, was right. We had to join forces with him and his gang. It was the only way we had a chance at surviving.

EVERY SECOND OR THIRD DAY OVER THE NEXT FEW MONTHS, my brothers and I would head out to the housing divisions and aim those metal chopsticks at the lowest beams of the fences, at the approximate height of a street kid's shins or knees. Against the old abandoned house that became our home for nearly a year, we aimed higher, as if going for a street kid's chest.

Big Brother didn't need to tell me, although he did anyway. The chopsticks were good only at a distance. So he put Min-gook in charge of building our endurance. Min-gook would have us run, barefoot, across the hills, marathon distances, in the heat of summer. And in fall, with sneakers on, we'd run the dirt paths that wove their way through the forests. We'd run the same paths in winter, our feet digging into the snow, adding extra tension to build up our muscles and strength.

Young-bum oversaw our weight-lifting training, using as weights small boulders he picked up in the fields. Big Brother and his gang started doing mock fights with us, during which I taught everyone tae kwon do kicks and punches. But mostly Big Brother taught us street fighting, including holds and how to bite. He and his crew also taught us some stealing techniques, like using two razors instead of one. By placing one razor flat, between our index and middle fingers, another between our index and thumb, we could make large holes, shaped like half-moons, in our victims' bags, allowing us to steal even more, maybe even the entire contents of a bag. In battle, of course, holding the razors like this could be deadly against a victim's throat.

We stole money for Big Brother and his gang, and by autumn, we were fighting other *kotjebi* gangs alongside them, too. All the fights were easy. We ruled Pohwang.

By winter solstice 1999, my brothers and I were strong, just as strong as the men. And certainly stronger than any of us had ever been in our lives. My chest muscles rippled like the waves on the sea, and my leg and arm muscles when flexed were hard as steel.

S tarting in the spring of 1999, every second month or so my gang and I returned to Gyeong-seong for a few days just to check in, to see if our parents had come back. On my first visit, I went to my house and asked the old man who now owned it if anyone had come looking for me. He stared at me through hazy blue eyes, as Young-bum's grandmother had. He opened his mouth to say something, but then the younger man stepped between us and pushed me away.

"If you ever return here, I'll call the *Shangmoo*," he said, kicking me in the rib cage. "Get out of here and never come back."

I could have fought him, that man who stole my house. A burning hatred grew inside me whenever I thought of him. I knew, though, that if I punched him, he would never help me. I needed to believe that if my mother returned, he would at least tell her I was a *kotjebi*, so she could look for me.

Whenever I returned to Gyeong-seong, I'd sneak up to my old house and spy on it from the back of a bush, hoping maybe my parents might come out instead of this other family.

We boys shared few of our experiences in Gyeong-seong other than letting one another know that our parents still had not returned. We all choked on the tears that we refused to share. It was hard to go back there. It was like walking into a grave.

My brothers and I did talk, though, about how we would give anything to have Myeongchul back, even if that meant working underneath another gang like Big Brother's. None of us cared that much anymore about winning. But looking after ourselves to make sure we didn't lose another gang member? That was my new goal. I would fight to my own death. I knew that now.

These thoughts were swirling in my mind when, in the fall, on a visit back to Gyeong-seong, we came face-to-face with Young-bum's old gang, the *Jjacdari-pa*. Spitting angry, they wanted an "all together" fight. The leader of *Jjacdari-pa*, the boy who had busted Young-bum's lip open and forced him to lose a tooth back when we were still all going to school, was like a smaller version of Big Brother. Big and hard. He also had piercing eyes that dug their way into Young-bum. I knew that look now. It meant *kill*.

It was as though Young-bum had done something to really offend him. But all he did was leave—or, rather, get kicked out—because he kept back some won to buy his grandmother medicine. Big Brother had taught me that when my opponents became emotional, that was weakness. Play on it. Make them angrier. So I did. I spat insults at the leader about how his gang didn't know how to fight, how mine had become fierce, how in kicking Young-bum out, the *Jjacdari-pa* had lost its only good fighter.

It worked, and our battle with the *Jjacdari-pa* was over in less than fifteen minutes. Every *Jjacdari-pa* member eventually ran off, the leader calling over his shoulder that they were heading to Rajin-Seonbong to take over the territory we refused to claim for ourselves.

I shook my head as he ran away and slung my arm around Young-bum.

"We should chase after him," Young-bum said.

"Nah, let him have the last word and Rajin-Seonbong. We have you."

IN THE SPRING OF 2000, MY BROTHERS AND I RETURNED from a trip to Gyeong-seong to find Big Brother and his gang gone. Their few things, including metal chopsticks and clothes, were all missing, too. Chulho and I figured that they'd been caught by the police or the *Shangmoo*. Or that they had just picked up and left for a better market. Either way, we weren't surprised. We assumed Big Brother was a target. The police don't take kindly to military dodgers. If caught, Big Brother would have been beaten, maybe even killed. Every male in Joseon must serve ten years in the army; females, seven years. I also knew that with Big Brother's disappearance, our safe house was no longer safe. The *Shangmoo* would come looking for us soon enough. We, too, had to leave.

We talked as a group and decided to head to Eodaejin, the sea, and conquer the market that we had given up a year earlier, perhaps a little too quickly. This time, we would be ready.

WE CAME INTO EODAEJIN MARKET FROM THE WEST AND ON the offensive, tossing metal chopsticks at the knees and thighs of all the *kotjebi* we saw. They keeled over in pain and shock and then asked us who we were. I told them Chang, and that we'd come from Pohwang. That was enough. Most had heard rumors about us, either from other *kotjebi* or merchants traveling from market to market. We were known as the gang who had defeated the Rajin-Seonbong boys and who had spent a year training with a man-gang. It took only a few days for Eodaejin Market to echo with fictionalized stories of our triumphs, including training sessions that involved our slaying wild boar with our bare hands and hurling nunchaku with such precision we could skin the fur off a bear.

I'd laugh when I'd hear these stories but then wonder after: Was this how Kim Il-sung's childhood snowballed into such an epic? Myeongchul's words came back to me: *Folklore has a funny way of becoming truth.*

One thing was certain. My gang and I had become legend.

¤ ¤ ¤

IF MYEONGCHUL WAS OUR VOICE, CHULHO WAS OUR EARS. He would spend hours drinking and smoking with the merchants and flirting with the women, all the while learning their problems and discovering information, including how Joseon rebounded from the great famine caused when the United States launched a nuclear weapon at our eastern shores. Depending on who was telling the story, either hundreds or tens of thousands of people were killed in that attack, and those left alive suffered from all sorts of diseases. The country was being invaded, but Joseon was winning because all our supplies were going to Pyongyang to help our army and navy.

"Do you believe this?" I asked Chulho one evening at the train station, where we were sleeping.

"I think it's just Pyongyang's way of taking all the country's food and *sool*," he replied slowly, as if admitting something to himself for the first time.

"But for the merchants who give you an egg, a piece of tofu, for you to listen to them, you'll believe anything, right?"

"Yeah," he replied. He then smiled. "Somewhere in the middle is the truth."

"Okay, but how do we know where the middle is?" Sangchul asked, joining us. He was nursing a wound on the palm of his hand. He had caught it on a metal fence while running away from a vendor.

"I have no idea," Chulho answered, "but maybe we can figure it out together." He looked at each of us. "Listen to the merchants. Most people talk and talk and talk and never hear a thing anyone else is saying. But try to really listen. Like when we bring food back every night to share with one another, try to bring home one story each to divvy up between us."

"Oh, speaking of merchants," Young-bum said, "they want us to work for them."

"Spit it out," Chulho said, facing Young-bum and folding his arms across his chest.

"Several of the fish vendors have asked if we could load and unload their crates and chase other *kotjebi* away," Young-bum explained. "In return, they'll give us food every day and some won if we don't steal from them."

"Just what Myeongchul wanted . . . a legitimate job," Unsik said in a hushed voice.

We all fell silent at the mention of his name.

"The merchants won't turn us in to the *Shangmoo* or the police?" Min-gook eventually asked.

"No. They assured me they wouldn't," Young-bum said. "They said we could steal from other vendors . . . enough that maybe we can survive through an entire winter if we save." He then turned and faced Sangchul directly. "They even asked me if any of us performed. I told them about you. If you want to sing for some extra won, sing. The merchants will let you stand on one of their boxes as a stage."

A quiet fell over us again. I don't know what the others were thinking, but I sure wished Myeongchul were around to perform, too.

MY BROTHERS AND I LIVED BY THE SEA IN A FISHING SHED that one of the merchants lent us.

During that summer of 2000, we spent our days in the market beating up other *kotjebi* and lugging fish, and our nights staring up at the sky and listening to the cackle of burning logs in Unsik's fires. I fell asleep to lullabies I swear I could hear coming off the sea, and woke to twisted bread being warmed on the bonfire.

I gained the confidence to speak to the vendors with whom I now worked, the way Chulho did. I would sit with these old sea-worn men on low stools around fires, waiting for customers, drinking *sool*, smoking their hand-rolled cigarettes, and listening, trying to really listen, to their stories.

The merchants told me that Joseon's prisons, particularly those near the border, were now bursting with women, many of whom were mothers, including pregnant women who were being forced to abort their fetuses.

What could pregnant women do to the government? I thought. What secrets did our mothers know to sell to the South or to America? But putting in my own opinion on things, Chulho had taught me, was not listening.

"Because the babies were conceived in China," one merchant

answered, as if reading my mind. "Maybe by Chinese husbands. Maybe by men from here but who have not lived in Joseon for a long time. Doesn't matter. Either way, Joseon now wants these babies dead. They're not pure North Koreans, you see."

"Children are supposed to be the kings and queens of Joseon," I finally quipped. What I was really thinking, though, was that my mother could be one of these women.

"It gets even worse," the merchant continued. "If someone from Joseon manages to make it through China to the South— Namjoseon—the government there will give them money and food, even a house to live in. Namjoseon will ask for all sorts of secrets and then, when all is said that is needed to be said, Joseon people are killed."

Everyone really did hate us, just as our eternal leader had always said. Maybe all along, the government was trying to protect us. Listening to the merchants made me more confused than ever. I didn't know whom to trust. Joseon really was an island on its own. And my parents? Where were they? I didn't even want to think about it. My gut hurt so bad from all the worry, I started drinking water all day long mixed with syrup made from the opium plant. It was the only thing that helped me forget on some days. On other days, *sool* was enough. And still on others, I had to beat someone up to feel as though I wasn't spiraling out of control.

A merchant who sold old refurbished radios told me that opium and alcohol were the gods of the streets. I had actually approached him wanting to buy one of his radios. I'd heard that new radios captured signals from Chinese, sometimes even Southern, stations. That's why, whenever my father was given a radio in Pyongyang, the government would put some device inside before he could bring it home, so the signals would be blocked, all signals except those from Joseon.

I left radio-less, with two bottles of *sool* instead.

"As a small child, I thought Kim Il-sung was a god," I told Sangchul on a lazy day in late summer as we floated in the waves of the sea, *sool* moving through my veins and making me tired, as I had started drinking in the morning. For a moment I felt the water cradling me the way the night sky seemed to do the earth. For a moment I had this experience in which I felt I was a star and someone far away was looking up at me. A calm moved through me, a peace I hadn't felt in a long time.

Sangchul wasn't saying anything.

"My father was kicked out of Pyongyang," I finally said.

"I know," he replied. "Why?"

"I have no idea. All he ever told me was that we were going on vacation. You know," I continued after a long silence, "I think the worst thing anyone can do to another human being isn't take away their home, their job, their parents. I think the worst thing anyone can do is make them stop believing in something higher, something good, something pure, a reason for everything—hope, maybe. God, maybe."

"Maybe hope and God are the same," he said dreamily.

"Maybe. And maybe the best oppressors know to take away our physical security, then our connection to loved ones, then hope, then dreams, and finally God dies along with everything else," I whispered. "Then we're dead until a savior comes along."

"Kim Il-sung was our savior," Sangchul said in a low voice.

"But who's going to save us from Kim Il-sung?" Chulho, swimming out to join us, chirped in.

"Maybe we can find ourselves a magic gourd to pull us all through?" I mumbled.

CHAPTER

23

very time any of us got a *shibwon,* we squirrelled it away in a plastic bag, which we hid under a stone near a birch tree. We wanted to save enough so that we could buy our food for the entire winter and not have to fight other *kotjebi* for the right to a part of a market to steal for it.

In the early fall of 2000, we finally dug out the bag and counted our money. We didn't have nearly what we wanted—maybe only enough to go a month without stealing, and even that was a stretch.

We needed more, so we started stealing from the government farms, stuffing corn, peppers, lettuce, cucumbers, potatoes, and even poppy seeds from the opium fields into our bags. We sold the produce to the merchants.

We wore black long-sleeved shirts and pants that made us sweat. But the clothing helped keep us unseen, especially on the darkest nights. We'd crawl through the fields, sometimes lying flat on our stomachs, using our elbows to pull us along. We needed to remain hidden from Worker Peasant Red Guards that doubled up when the first crops started to be harvested.

One time, when a full moon lit us up, I stifled a laugh looking around at all of us. We looked like a special ops unit. "My childhood dream was to lead a paramilitary group like us," I reminded my brothers. "But instead of laying bombs, scoping out enemy territory, maybe even acting as snipers . . ."

"We're stealing carrots," Young-bum finished the sentence for me.

"I guess dreams do come true," Chulho scoffed.

It wasn't that hard to rob the government farms, at least at first. The Worker Peasant Red Guards didn't seem well organized. It was easy to sneak past them.

As a result, I grew cocky, and perhaps that was my downfall.

One night, some of the guards caught my brothers and me when I thought it would be safe to just walk onto a farm.

They beat us with long sticks and locked all of us in an airless shed, which was so small and cramped we couldn't really move much.

I choked on the stench of manure, which, when the moon spilled in through the windows, I could see was piled from floor to ceiling in a corner of the shed in tin buckets stacked one on top of the other. In the morning, black and blue, we were told we had two choices: Spread the manure on the fields as fertilizer or go to the *guhoso*.

I dry-heaved because I had no food or water in me to throw up, and not just from the foul stench. Some of the manure, the guards boasted, had been taken from the outhouses at the prisons. The manure was a mix of animal and human waste.

While my brothers and I worked, the guards chewed gum, smoked our cigarettes, and followed us to make sure we didn't run away.

CHULHO ARRIVED BACK AT THE SHED BY THE SEA ONE EVEning in the fall of 2000, announcing in a singsong voice that he had heard that in the nearby town of Hwaseong was a farm called Ilho. A merchant had proposed a deal: If we stole its only product, pears, we could keep half the stock for ourselves to eat or sell at other markets. For the other half, the merchant would give us thirty won per kilogram—enough, Chulho beamed, that we could coast through the winter months.

"We have to take this job," Chulho said, dancing around Unsik's fire. He was drunk. "We can find a safe, warm place to live and just, well, rest through the winter."

I know this farm, I thought to myself as Chulho chattered on about his plan to steal the pears. Each fall in Pyongyang, my father would come home with a box of pears that he said were from Hwaseong. The pears were large, honey-colored, and dripping in syrup that slipped down my chin and stained my shirts when I ate them.

"These are pears for our general," I interrupted Chulho. "They're for Kim Jong-il and the Pyongyang elite."

Chulho swatted me across the forehead. "Can you listen?" he spat. "I'm talking."

"No," I cut in. "Your plan is too risky. These are prized pears, the nectars of the gods. I have this sinking feeling. I don't want to do this one."

Chulho slapped me across the head again. "Get a grip!" he yelled. "If we can get enough pears, we can go back to Gyeong-seong and Young-bum's house. If the house has been sold, we can buy it back with the profits from the pears. We can wait for our parents there. Stealing these pears is our ticket to a new life."

I was outvoted. Everyone wanted to follow Chulho to Ilho. Of course, I would never allow my brothers to go anywhere without me. If anyone was going to die in battle, I had vowed it would be me, so I tagged along, too. With every step, though, I had this terrible feeling that we were walking into a trap.

WE HAD TO WAIT SEVERAL DAYS IN THE STATION FOR A train headed to Hwaseong, and the night one came, the clouds sank on top of the mountains, covering their peaks. There was that stillness in the air, that omen of a storm.

When we arrived in Ilho, the first thing my brothers and I did was find a safe place, an old wood log off the side of the road in the middle of a cluster of evergreens, where we would meet up if we got separated.

We then slid up toward one of the pear farms and hid ourselves in some haystacks in a neighboring field. I peered out through a tiny hole I made in the straw, studying the guards as they marched back and forth. I was searching for a break in their routine—a window to steal our way into the pear trees.

Nothing.

These Worker Peasant Red Guards were well organized and well prepared for thieves.

But the night guards, the two who came on shortly before midnight, were different. They were definitely locals, with hard accents and even harder, dirtier appearances. They were tired—I could tell by their sluggish gait—and stayed close to the outskirts of the farm, rather than weaving in and out of the trees the way the day guards did. One night guard carried a rifle, but I knew from my father that only the State Security Agency, the police of the federal government, ever had guns with real bullets. The State Security Agency wore a different uniform than these men, and it didn't care about farming. The *Shangmoo*, the police, and the Worker Peasant Red Guards who did care were never given real ammunition.

Under the battery-operated spotlight, which swooped into the pear trees and then out again, I could see that the other guard carried a wooden gun painted to look real, much like the weapon my father had made for me when I was a child.

Every hour, right to the second, the two men took breaks behind a pillar to share a cigarette.

The spotlight, I also observed, didn't dig itself in deep enough to reach the center of the trees, which had been planted in neat rows, pruned to look like soldiers standing at attention.

"Here's the plan," I whispered to the others. "When the guards are smoking, with their backs turned, and the spotlight has begun its circle to the west of the trees, run, and run fast and far. Count out two minutes, then lie flat on your stomachs with your hands and feet stretched out. Watch for the spotlight then. It should float over you, because it floats across the periphery of the trees every two minutes. Right when the spotlight has left you, run again for two minutes and then lie flat again. The third time you do this, the spotlight won't reach you. Start picking the pears. You should be about in the center of the trees and able to pick as much as you want with no one noticing. When done, make your way back out the same way you went in, until you are close enough to see the guards again. When they go for a smoke, leave and head to the safe place."

The problem, though, was that we were all salivating at the thought of the taste of sweetness. I'd been hiding in the haystacks for hours, and my legs were cramped and hurt. My entire body tingled from a lack of circulation. Unsik told me later that he was imagining baking the pears on the bonfire with chocolate. Young-bum was planning to eat a pear right on the spot.

We were overeager and took off running just as the one guard lit up the smoke but before the other had made it behind the pillar.

Min-gook, Chulho, and Young-bum were fast and hadn't seen our error. I was behind them and saw it all. The guards caught Unsik and Sangchul before the boys even made it into the trees. I managed to sneak into the orchard and hide behind a tree trunk. I watched the guards wrestle Unsik and Sangchul to the ground, then tie rope around their wrists. The guards then dragged my brothers across the stone path to their shed.

For a moment I felt paralyzed, not knowing what to do. Then I started to swear under my breath. We'd promised, we'd all made a vow that we would never leave anyone behind. Maybe everything had been taken from us, but we still had our word, and that meant something. I wouldn't betray my brothers.

Still swearing, I ran until I caught up to Chulho, Min-gook, and Young-bum, who, being fast, were in the center of the farm with their bags already bursting with pears by the time I reached them.

Breathless, I told them what had happened.

Chulho shook his head, spat, and swore, too.

"We made a pact," Min-gook said.

"I know," I whispered.

We dropped our bags and walked with our heads lowered,

shuffling our feet, back toward the guards, our hands in the air to indicate our surrender. There was no point in trying to fight the guards to get our friends back. They were powerful men to begin with, but even if we overpowered them, the police and the *Shangmoo* would hunt us down until they found us. We had only one choice: Turn ourselves in.

THE GUARDS DIDN'T BEAT US. THEY LOCKED US FOR THE night in the shed, which luckily didn't have any manure in it.

In the morning, they walked us to the *guhoso*.

When we entered the main gate, we saw some *kotjebi* sweeping and others chopping wood with axes, all of them watched over by guards. There were two long buildings for the *kotjebi*: one for males, the other for females. When I walked, or rather, when the guards pushed me, into the building for us boys, I immediately saw the torn gray wool blankets piled in the corner, which moved with lice and other bugs. Four boys lay on the ground wrapped in some of these blankets, lifeless, like Young-bum's grandmother when I first met her. It was raining, and as I moved into the room, droplets of water dripped on me from the holes in the roof.

The kids in the *guhoso* ranged in age from ten to eighteen, which made me wonder where the little ones went. But I didn't have time to answer that question. My brothers and I tried to get out, of course, on our very first night there. But we discovered that the planks of wood nailed over the windows had been nailed so tight we'd need a tool to jimmy them open. We were trying to pick the lock in the only door with a piece of metal Chulho had smuggled into the prison in his mouth when the manager and some guards unlocked it for us. As punishment for trying to escape, the *guhoso* manager tied Unsik to a pole, the way the police tied prisoners waiting for execution, in the center of the *guhoso* yard. For that night and the following day, Unsik wasn't allowed to eat, drink, or use the toilet. By the time he was let loose, he reeked of his own excrement.

After that . . . well, we never got much sleep, any of us. For one, there was no room to lie down, so we slept sitting up, cross-legged, leaning against one another. The older *kotjebi* made the youngest boys sleep near the drafty door and windows. The younger ones had coughs, moaned and cried, and urinated on us all night long. In the day, I could see that the little ones were so malnourished that their skin hung from their bodies like oversize T-shirts, but their stomachs shot out in front of them like they were pregnant women. I soon discovered why. When our meals came—twice a day—the older boys took all the food, which was pretty much always rotten potatoes, moldy and soft and covered in flies. The little ones were given the leftovers, which weren't much. Simply put, the older boys in the *guhoso*, many of whom were part of gangs, were killing the younger ones.

I was also kept awake by the girls in the other building moaning and groaning. Even though we were separated, I still knew what was going on. Sex, lots of it. I may have left Pyongyang an innocent boy, believing that holding a girl's hand meant marriage and then babies. But I knew now that sex trailed poverty like alcohol. And girls—well, they had it bad if they were good-looking. That's why during the day many of the girls hid in the back of the jail, cutting their lips with sharp sticks and pulling out their hair. They wanted to be ugly, so the guards wouldn't choose them.

A few mornings each week, I'd awake to stare into the open eyes of a child, usually the youngest, who had died in the night. I kid you not, but sometimes in that place just before awakening, I'd see that dead boy walking among us, no longer sickly but alive and sparkling like the sun on the crest of a wave. He would see me, wave, as if waiting for me to say goodbye, and then leave . . . *up*, like a balloon full of helium on Parade Day.

"We've become murderers," I whispered to Chulho one night. "The state is clever. We'll kill each other before ever defying them."

EVERY MORNING, WE STOOD OUTSIDE IN SINGLE-FILE LINES, like we had done at school, while the *guhoso* manager did work selections. He sent some kids to clean the toilets, others to the mountains to find kindling and firewood. A few were sent to help cook in the kitchen, which basically meant skinning the potatoes, boiling them, and when not doing that, cutting wood. Some boys were also sent out to pick up *kotjebi* who had died in the market and bury them in the hills. I'd seen them do this from the other side, the freedom side. Not realizing at the time that these were *guhoso* boys, I'd see these kids, watched over by guards, lug the stiff bodies from the market in old rickety wooden wheelbarrows.

What I picked up pretty quickly was that the *guhoso* manager had a racket going on. He sent the strongest *kotjebi* gang to Hwaseong Market to steal cigarettes and money for him and the other guards. At first, my brothers and I all slunk to the very back and scrunched our shoulders down to avoid being picked. None of us wanted to work for these *guhoso* skinny pigs, who would drink the alcohol that had been stolen for them at night, chain-smoke, and play card games like *sasakki*. These guards, when really drunk, would stagger and fall over us, looking for and calling out the names of the pretty girls. They were lost in their stupor and had come to the boys' building instead.

I hated the smell of them. All of them.

One day, however, the manager with a wide, pockmarked face chose Young-bum to go to the market. I guess something about the gang the manager had been using had ticked him off, because when he stood at the front, his eyes floated over his usual boys and went straight to Young-bum.

I had to be quick on my feet, because I didn't want Young-bum to refuse and be hung out on the pole, because that's what the guards did with any kid who said no to their work duty. I also didn't want Young-bum to go alone to the market or, worse, with the other gang, who surely, when the guards weren't looking, would beat him up for interfering with their work.

I flung my hand high in the air and waved it at the manager. A guard dragged me out of the line and up to the front. When we stood face-to-face, the manager spat saliva onto my cheek. "What do you want, street boy?" he croaked.

Wiping my face with my sleeve, I told him about our gang, how we were one of the best. "We're fast on our feet," I boasted. I then told the manager that if he didn't believe me, to ask the merchants, because everyone in markets far and wide had heard of me and my gang.

The man looked at me with his beady eyes, which gave me the shivers. I saw nothing human inside him. "I know who you are," he finally said. "Everyone does. *Chang-pa*, the most feared gang in the province. I was testing you when I picked your street brother. I've been waiting for your gang to volunteer. My old boys have become weak. The merchants now hide their things from them. I want new blood . . . yours."

I inhaled deeply, thinking here was our chance to escape. We could overtake the guards at the market.

"Except you, him, and him," the *guhoso* manager said, pointing to me, Unsik, and Sangchul. "You three remain behind as collateral to make sure your gang will come back. I know"—he leaned over, his breath smelling of fish paste and day-old alcohol—"I know how you operate. You'll never leave anyone behind."

Before Young-bum left for the market, I pulled him aside. "You need to bring as much stuff as you can—including won, alcohol, desserts . . . whatever you can steal—back to this bastard, because my plan is to gain his trust. I want us, and us alone, to steal for him from now on. We will become invaluable to him so that he gives us extra food, and then somehow, when he is not looking, we'll run away."

MY BROTHERS RETURNED AT THE END OF THE DAY WITH bags full of cigarettes and alcohol, including the pricey and hard-to-find *takjoo*, North Korean rice wine.

The manager stuffed a twisted bread stick into his mouth and, spitting crumbs everywhere, announced in front of all the boys that he had made the lineup again, that from that day on, my boys, and my boys alone, would go to the market.

Being the *guhoso* manager's favorite didn't mean life was good for us, though. Sure, he didn't make me, Unsik, and Sangchul do chores. I no longer got toilet duty, which meant loading our feces into buckets and carrying them to the oxcart for other boys to take to the farms to be spread as fertilizer by yet other boys captured while trying to raid the farms. I also didn't have to scrub the buckets afterward with pebbles in the cold river.

But we didn't get any extra food. And the other *kotjebi* gangs in the *guhoso* didn't like that we were all of a sudden the *it* boys. Four guys jumped me when I was alone one afternoon circling the *guhoso* grounds, getting exercise. The skin over my rib cage was bruised blue from being kicked so much and so hard in the same spot, and it hurt to breathe. At night, the other *kotjebi* gangs knew to stay away because my gang was all there to protect me, but by day, Unsik, Sangchul, and I were free game. And as the leader of the gang, I was the main target. Whenever the other boys had a chance, they would kick me in the groin or back, punch me in the stomach, and poke me in the eyes.

Sangchul, Unsik, and I started volunteering to do chores again, begging to collect wood on the mountain. Because we had to spread out, the manager always assigned extra guards for this duty. Every night, Young-bum would sneak me a pack of cigarettes and some bread, which I'd slip the next day to a guard to let Unsik, Sangchul, and me stay close to him to act as our heavy, to keep the other gang members away.

One day, about a month after we arrived, the manager called Young-bum and me into his office. "I'm going to send you and your guys to the special forces unit. You can become military. You are the bravest boys I've ever met," he told us.

"When?" Young-bum asked, wide-eyed and eager. We both had discussed that it was just a matter of time before the merchants got to know who we were and started hiding their goods when my boys walked into the market. Then the *guhoso* manager would move on to a new gang and we'd miss the opportunity, whatever it was, to escape.

"Next week," the manager said, beaming. I didn't believe him, though. For one, I knew as the son of a father in the military that the military only allows kids starting at the age of eighteen to begin their mandatory service. No child can start younger than that. I was fourteen. Chulho, our eldest, was fifteen.

So, of course, that next week turned into next month. Youngbum and the market crew were getting exhausted stealing as much as they were to make the guards happy.

My gang and I were more trapped than ever.

aybe because of the darker days that came as we approached the winter solstice, the night guards began to drink more and more. When they did, they became brutal, coming in and beating us kids for no reason and taking more of the girls. The girls, when I saw them the next day . . . Well, let's just say something about them had left. They looked out with eyes that seemed to be coated in frost, blinking slowly, as if they were living in a place where time moved backward. They wouldn't tell anyone where they'd been. But I knew. Street girls became *yu-ryeong*. Street boys became dragons breathing fire until they got themselves killed.

One morning I found a guard passed out on the ground outside our door, his face stuck to a thin layer of frost. It dawned on me as I watched him drooling and grumbling in his drunken sleep state that there was a way we could escape.

I flicked my fingers at Young-bum, indicating I wanted to have a meeting. He trailed behind me as I walked around the circumference of the building, as if getting some exercise. Around the back and away from the guards, I whispered my idea to him.

THAT NIGHT, WHEN THE GUARDS LOCKED US IN OUR BUILD-ing, my boys and I started phase one of my plan. Earlier in the day, Sangchul had scoffed a long, slim piece of metal from the garbage. Chulho and I used it to pull out the nails across the window, but it was hard. The nails were in tight. It took us several hours, in fact. Light was just starting to stream in through the window when all the nails were loosened.

That day, my brothers stole more alcohol from the Hwaseong Market than they ever had. They also stole food, including dried fish and clams.

When the manager saw it all, his greed came well before his responsibilities, just as I had hoped. He jumped up and down and clapped, his jowls flapping like flags. He shouted: "Tomorrow is a day off for the *kotjebi*. Tonight, we will have a festival."

The manager let my gang and me stay out past the usual time to pass the food and alcohol around. By midnight, the guards and manager were rip-roaring drunk, singing revolutionary songs at the top of their lungs.

The guards eventually passed out one by one, in such synchro-nicity it was like watching the close of a performance at the Mass

Games in the Rungrado Stadium in Pyongyang. That's when the *guhoso* manager locked us boys in our building for the night. But my gang and I stayed awake and listened to the manager stumbling around, trying to wake the other guards to get them to drink with him.

"'The roll of thunder at Kim Jong-il's peak,'" he sang in a booming baritone voice.

"How many *kotjebi* does it take to change a lightbulb?" he then called out.

"Four," he replied, since all the guards were asleep. "Because you're all so stupid!" He then threw rocks against the outside wall of our building.

Finally, I heard his body fall to the ground with a thud.

Then I heard his snoring, which was almost as loud as his singing.

My boys and I pulled the plank away from the window. We then pushed open the glass and jumped out.

We climbed over the wooden fence and ran at full speed, side by side, down the dirt road, not stopping until we reached the train station.

WE GOT OFF AT GILJU, WHERE WE DECIDED WE WERE ALL too weak after our stay in the *guhoso* to fight against other *kotjebi*. The best way to survive the winter would be to surrender to the first gang we faced. We would work for them.

The gang we met was called *Kim-pa*, and it had strong fighters; some even knew tae kwon do. They'd been homeless for a long time, but they hadn't developed any real strategies to steal. My gang taught them our techniques, including how to whistle and use sign language in the market to communicate orders to one another. I also taught them the importance of having two homes and how to communicate by laying a certain number of stones. "If, for example, there are three pebbles placed in a spot you all agree on—and it must be a spot hidden away, so the police and other gangs can't mess with it—it means that one of your brothers has come back and found it too dangerous to stay. Maybe the police or the *Shangmoo* are sniffing around, or another gang has taken over the place. Three pebbles means to go to the other safe place," I explained to their leader, Kim.

"Where did you learn all this?" he asked.

"When I was a child, I played army with my father and sometimes my mother. We would reenact many of Kim Il-sung's great battles against the Japanese, especially the one near Bocheonbo Mountain."

The *Kim-pa* had been in Gilju for a year and worked for many of the merchants. Because we were part of *Kim-pa*, these vendors shielded us when the police or the *Shangmoo* came. Some of the merchants even said we were their very own kids and not *kotjebi*. The vendors let Sangchul sing on New Year's and on Kim Jong-il's birthday on February 16.

I need to say that, despite all of our hard living—cigarettes; alcohol; bad, rotten food; opium—Sangchul's voice was still magnificent. His falsetto was a cascading waterfall that softened even the most hardened hearts. "In the valley where there are no tigers, the fox is king," I imagined Myeongchul would have said after this winter.

Indeed, in Gilju, we had no predators.

Our first mistake was moving on.

IN THE SPRING OF 2001, WE LEFT GILJU, LANDING IN KIM-chaek, mostly by accident because we had hopped the first train headed out of the station, not realizing it was going south when we wanted to go north. While Kimchaek was on the coast, which I liked, we didn't stay long. There was little food, for one. Kimchaek was the closest sea city to Pyongyang that we'd visited, and I think most of its food, particularly fish, was going to the capital. We stuck around the train station waiting to go somewhere else. One *kotjebi* told us the tracks were being repaired. Another said there was no electricity. Whatever the reason, there were just no trains running anywhere.

Our nights were spent in total darkness. None of the people living in the train station dared light a candle, a pinecone dipped in resin, or a kerosene lamp, fearing the police would see and raid the place. So my brothers and I found ourselves huddling close together, dodging bats and drunken men falling on top of us. The room stank of waste, for no one dared leave in the night to go outside and use a toilet. There were some women who sashayed around the station whispering, "Do you want a nightflower?"

I certainly knew now what was going on.

"I died a long time ago," a woman, who I was pretty sure was one of the nightflowers, told Chulho on our third day. I glanced quickly at her and then away, not wanting to embarrass her. I got enough of a look to know she'd been pretty once, with full lips and round eyes. Her hair was frizzy, but she looked clean. "I was sent to Rodong-dal-ryondae," she said, her voice faltering at the mention of Joseon's main prison, where few ever left alive, or so I had been told.

I came to realize then that everyone had a story. Everyone was affected by the famine—everyone outside Pyongyang, that is. I sometimes felt, listening to people tell their stories to Chulho, that there was a competition to see whose story was worst.

I got up, not wanting to hear this woman's sad tale, and walked to the other side of the station, where a young street girl, maybe my age, fifteen now, was rubbing a tin cup with a dirty rag. I'd been watching her since we arrived. She made me think of the orchid Kimilsungia, bred special for our eternal leader, with her watery black eyes set in the center of her bright, oval-shaped face. Something stirred inside me. Something fresh and light when I thought of her.

"Can I sit beside you?" I asked, lighting up a cigarette. By now,

I was chain-smoking so much that my fingertips had turned yellow.

"Yes," she said in a voice that chilled me like the winter wind, for she had the accent of Pyongyang.

"Are you from the capital?" I asked as I knelt down beside her. She really didn't need to answer. I knew. What I really wanted to know was, had she been forced to leave, too? I had believed for so long that my family was the only one. So far, I'd never met another *kotjebi* from Pyongyang.

"This world is not for the living anymore. Tread lightly, for all the dragons now fall," she said in a steely voice, which made the hair on the back of my neck stand on end the way the *yu-ryeong* did.

"You're a seer!" I exclaimed with a gasp.

The young woman turned to face me. Her complexion was smooth, and the whites in her eyes were bright. She wasn't suffering from malnutrition, at least not yet. Her brown irises had yellow dots, like a spiral pathway lined in candles.

"I left my body a long time ago," she continued in a soft, low voice. "Now I can only see the dead. And there is death around you."

I swallowed hard. "Are you sure?" I then shook my head and admonished myself. *I don't believe in fortune-tellers,* I scolded myself. *They sell folk stories, not facts.*

"I see you going to the South," she continued, ignoring my

question. "I see a hand taking yours." She then smiled. "I see you becoming a teacher. But before this happens . . . you need to remember to tread lightly, for all the dragons now fall."

"She's crazy. Don't listen to her," an old woman said, coming up behind me and pushing me to get up. I dusted my pants off as the old woman sat down beside the girl.

"Go," the old lady said in a creaky voice, like a rusted door hinge. "This girl has been hit in the head and knows nothing anymore."

WE FINALLY TOOK A TRAIN TO EORANG, JUMPING FROM the car when the train was still in motion. I landed hard, sending a shock through me, and rolled until I came to a stop in some mud. That was definitely an omen of what was to come. The merchants at Eorang Market beat us with clubs and told us to go away. They refused to discuss any arrangements for us to watch their stalls in exchange for food. One man told us we were all wild and crazy and couldn't be trusted. I wanted to tell the merchants about the gang in Rajin-Seonbong Market. Now, those boys *were* wild and crazy, high on the drug nicknamed ice that they got somewhere from someone who was importing it from China. This drug was made in laboratories and not grown in fields like our opium. But the merchants all plugged their ears, not wanting to talk to us at all.

The Eorang Market gangs were not strong, and we knew we could take them and take control of the merchants by fighting back. But we needed a few weeks of training, running the hills, lifting stones, mock fights with one another. We had become soft as kings in Gilju. We needed to become warriors again, the way Big Brother trained us, and refind that hunger that became fuel that we used to conquer foes. We decided that until we were ready, we would steal from the government farms instead of fight for territory in the market.

What I didn't know then was that we had all become dragons, too sure of ourselves and too coddled. We weren't as sharp as we had been. This was to prove to be our fatal flaw.

We headed out of the city on foot, the sun setting behind us, walking along the dirt roads, which eventually became mud paths weaving in and out of the hills of Orang County in North Hamgyeong Province. The air was fresh and filled with the scents of pine and cedar. No matter which direction we looked there were mountains.

"There is a rock somewhere near a river around here," Chulho said, "that the locals say brings good fortune. Make a wish at the rock, and it comes true."

"How does it do that?" Young-bum asked.

"Some spirit lives inside it."

"*Shan-shin-ryong-nim*," I whispered.

"You know it?" asked Young-bum.

"I've heard of the spirit," I replied.

"Follow me," Chulho said, walking out in front.

"Where?" I asked.

"Up there," he said, pointing to a nearby mountain and rock face that stretched up for hundreds of meters, with slopes and slabs that made me think of the story of Kim Il-sung's daring march, the *Learning Journey of a Thousand Miles*.

"That story was folklore, you know," I said to Chulho, who had already started to climb.

"What story?" he called out.

"The one in which Kim Il-sung walked as a child from China to North Korea. It was made up to make us think he was a god. You know," I continued, watching Chulho's technique, "you're as good a climber as any mountain goat. From now on, I nickname you 'Ram'!"

It took us a couple of hours to clamber up the mountain, digging our hands into the *huecos* to pull ourselves up, thrusting our bare toes into the crevices to give us support. But it was worth it. When we finally reached the top, it was as if we were gods looking down. From this vantage point, Joseon looked like a painting worthy of the halls of Pyongyang's finest buildings, a painting of swaying fields and tall evergreen forests framed by mountains. The sky was dyed pink and orange by the setting sun.

I could see for miles, including the government fields that lay low below us in the valley. Looking at the fields from up here was like looking at the stars from the sand: I felt everything was in order. Innocent. Pure. Peaceful.

The mountain had a flat top with two large polished patina boulders set side by side, touching each other.

I couldn't help but think as I closed my eyes and felt the sun on my face that this place had been built by a hand reaching down from the stars, putting things just so. Maybe that was how the lake in Baekdu Mountain had been formed.

WE LIVED AT THE ORANG TRAIN STATION PART-TIME, AND every few days we headed to the sea to bathe in the warm water.

We stole by night—potatoes, carrots, and cucumbers—which we sold at the market for food, *sool*, and cigarettes. The merchants soon began to trust us and left their goods out, knowing we were buying not stealing. And the other market gangs, fearing our reputation, left us alone.

At the end of the potato season that year, 2001, when I was confident we had this town, I had a dream that disturbed me to my core.

Young-bum's grandmother was in it, wearing a long white dress. She was years younger than she was when she died. She was beautiful—breathtaking, even. She didn't look at me, though. She was crossing a river, walking on water, carrying in her arms a boy dressed in black. I could not see the child's face. She disappeared on the other side of the river in some bulrushes.

I awoke, panting, the words of the young seer I had met at the train station in Kimchaek playing over and over in my mind: *This world is not for the living anymore. Tread lightly, for all the dragons now fall.*

I WAS STILL THINKING ABOUT THE DREAM WHEN WE STOLE our way onto a government potato farm.

The guards had caught another *kotjebi* gang earlier in the evening and were beating them in the shed. We could hear the boys' screams moving across the fields with us. Their capture allowed us to go unnoticed.

As I plucked potatoes and stuffed them into my bag, I heard a fist or a bat or something hit hard flesh and bone. For a moment I stopped what I was doing and looked around. Chulho, digging, hissed for me to get a move on.

Then I saw a light dance across the crops.

I stopped what I was doing and crouched down low.

It was Chulho, not Unsik, who gave three long whistles, meaning danger, time to leave and quick.

I whisked my bag onto my shoulder and ran at top speed, weaving in and out of the crops, hoping to lose anyone who might be on my trail. As I drew near our safe spot, though, something made me stop. I whistled for Chulho and Min-gook, who were up ahead, to come back as Sangchul and Unsik pulled up alongside me.

"Where is Young-bum?" I said, breathing heavily, catching my breath.

"Maybe in there." Min-gook motioned to some nearby pine trees.

I looked up at the sky, which was cloudless. The stars seemed to shine brighter than I'd ever seen them before. The constellation Ursa Major was directly above me. I stared at the brightest star, Chilseong, and all her children that made up the Big Dipper.

Chulho tugged on my sleeve, trying to get me to run. But I brushed his hand away. "They have Young-bum. I know they do," I said.

"We need to get out of here or else we're all going back to the *guhoso*," Min-gook said.

"Trust me. I heard . . . I heard . . . *I heard* . . ." I was stammering now, my thoughts moving quickly, the way Min-gook ran.

"What did you hear?" Chulho demanded.

"The sound of a club on flesh," I finally managed to get out. "The sound didn't come from the shed where the guards were beating the other *kotjebi*. The sound came from outside."

Once again, the seer's words came to me: *This world is not for the living anymore. Tread lightly, for all the dragons now fall.*

"Something bad has happened," I said in a hushed voice. "I know it. I need to go back."

I WALKED TOWARD THE MAIN BUILDING OF THE FARM, crouching low in the crops in the hopes that maybe, just maybe, I was wrong and the guards didn't have Young-bum. Then, if the guards didn't see me, I could scamper away once I knew we were all safe.

The screams from the shed had stopped. As I drew near, all I heard coming from inside was the sound of muffled whimpering. I swallowed hard, knowing the guards had abandoned torturing the other gang to look for us.

Suddenly, a light shone in my face. I stood up tall on shaky legs and raised my hands into the air.

"Get out of here," a gruff voice said to me.

The flashlight moved from me to a guard who was holding up Young-bum. Young-bum's head hung down and loose, as if he were a puppet whose handler was waiting to go onstage.

"Take your friend with you," the guard growled.

I moved cautiously toward Young-bum, half expecting to be walking into a trap. But neither guard moved to capture me as I lifted up Young-bum's face and studied his wounds. Blood dripped from his mouth, eyes, and nose.

The guard carrying Young-bum pushed him into my arms, turned, and walked away.

I must have been a giant that night, for I lifted Young-bum onto my shoulders and walked with wide, strong steps across the potato field. I didn't stop when I saw the others, who were waiting for me. I didn't stop at the pine trees, bundled together as if a child had planted them. I marched until I reached the Orang River, where I laid the moaning Young-bum, seeping blood onto my clothes and mumbling sentences I could not make out, on the sand on the bank.

My brothers soon joined me, kneeling by Young-bum's side the way they had when Myeongchul was hurt.

Unsik passed me a pinecone smeared with resin, which I lit with my trembling hands, not really wanting to see the full extent of Young-bum's wounds. I bit my lip to stop myself from screaming out loud when I could see. The entire right side of Young-bum's neck was bloodied and blue, soft like paper floating on the sea. I felt that if I touched it, it would break into a thousand bits and disintegrate.

Young-bum's breathing was short and raspy, like his grandmother's before she died.

I quickly tore off my shirt and had Unsik dip it into the water. I then patted down Young-bum's burning face.

Unsik held one of Young-bum's hands. I held the other, while Sangchul shone the pinecone up for all of us to see.

Young-bum opened his mouth, but his voice was too faint to hear. Wheezing with the effort, he twisted my hand around and pulled me down close to him.

"Go find your families," he said in such a quiet voice that I had to repeat the sentence for the others to know what he had said.

"When you find my father, do not tell him I died. Just say I left the group."

"You're not going to die," I started to protest, but he pinched my hand hard.

He seemed to smile, and for a moment his entire face looked sun-kissed, as it did when we lived on the beach in Eodaejin. His eyes looked like dew drops sitting on leaves in the morning. He didn't look at me. Or anyone else, for that matter. He just stared out, into nothing, and stopped blinking.

Stopped breathing.

His hand in mine fell lifeless.

I started to cry, as if all those other times I wanted to weep, the pain had just collected on the other side of a big dam. This, however, was the final blow that broke it. All my grief exploded.

I gathered Young-bum into my arms and just held him, crying into him, not letting go.

"You're my brother!" I screamed, my voice echoing against the large boulders near the river. "We're a team. You can't go!" But like that very first day when Young-bum had taken me to the market, he had already left before I could finish what I wanted to tell him.

The others crowded around Young-bum's body and me. No one could sleep. No one said a word for the longest time.

At last I said, "My grandfather told me that love burns brighter than any star, so bright that love can be seen and felt from one end of the earth to the other. One day, when those children on other planets see our dead earth, it will be your light they see, not Kim Il-sung's or Kim Jong-il's. But the light of people like you."

The owls called and the beetles and tiny insects pitter-pattered around me on their suction-cupped feet. At the darkest part of the night, I saw those lights again, blue and white, moving south with the wind. The *shan-shin-ryong-nim*.

I then heard my heartbeat, followed by distant bells.

Young-bum had arrived wherever it was he was supposed to go.

MY BROTHERS AND I STAYED WITH YOUNG-BUM'S BODY FOR two days, singing and talking to him, all of us, as if he were still there. I bathed his stiff body in the river, washing away all the blood. I combed his hair with a brush I made from sticks. I then placed him in my own T-shirt, so he would remember me.

Chulho found the rock that some peasants said was home to *shan-shin-ryong-nim*. On the third day, at the base of that rock, we dug with our hands a shallow grave for Young-bum and laid his body in it.

The boys and I roasted potatoes and found *gamtae*, a wild berry that Young-bum liked to eat, often fistfuls at a time. We set these on large ferns as plates for Young-bum to take to the afterworld.

Young-bum's death was a turning point for me, and not a positive one.

I'd been on the streets for more than three years. My *kotjebi* gang, *Chang-pa*, which had started out as seven, was now five.

Our voice, Myeongchul, went first, followed by our heart, Young-bum. I was angry, bitter, and full of so much sorrow that I found the only way to cope was to seal myself off from feeling. I consumed *sool* like water at the end of a dry day. Anytime a memory popped into my mind, I'd smoke a cigarette, take another sip of alcohol, or fight to get it to go away.

If a *kotjebi* in the Orang Market, where we lived for several months, brushed my arm, I turned on him with such rage, he didn't know what hit him. He'd be down, kicked, and punched before he could even lift an arm to fight back. I became everything the merchants thought I was before I arrived, if not worse. I searched for ice, asking everyone coming from out of town if they knew where I could find some. I knew I'd take it until I reached heaven, if God would let me in.

Sure, I still had dreams of my parents, but I'd always tell myself sometime during the dream that I was just having a nightmare. My parents were gone, likely dead, and I was an abandoned street child.

THEN ONE MORNING BY THE TRAIN STATION WHERE I WAS sleeping, as some magpies woke me with their haughty chatter, I heard Young-bum whisper to me: "Go back to Gyeong-seong." I awoke, startled, thinking for a moment that he was still alive and that the past few months had just been a dream.

I had this burning determination inside me to honor that promise to Young-bum to find his father and tell him that his son was brave and kind and the best friend I ever had. He was my brother. I needed to tell him that Young-bum had simply just left the group.

Chulho, Unsik, Min-gook, and Sangchul felt it was time to go back to Gyeong-seong, too. We'd been gone now for more than a year and a half, enough time that surely some of our parents had returned.

So that's how we ended up back there in the middle of the harvest season in 2001, at the Gyeong-seong train station, standing on the platform near the grassy knoll where Sangchul used to sing and Myeongchul would act, searching every face for our mothers and fathers.

SOON ENOUGH, THOUGH, WE DISCOVERED THAT NOT ONLY were our parents not there and hadn't ever returned but also that the *so-nyon-dan* manager, the teacher, our neighbors . . . all had gone, too.

Even the merchants had changed.

It was as if our families had never existed.

It was as if *I* had never existed. My mind started to play tricks on me, especially when I was drunk, that maybe we'd returned to the wrong town. Maybe this wasn't even Gyeong-seong. Maybe we were actually dead and this was the land in between.

One person was still there, though: the old woman who sold nightflowers. Long lost were my and my brothers' morals around the selling of women. For every male customer we brought the old lady, we were given ten won, enough to buy two steamed buns or ten candies. Sometimes we collected as many as six men in a night and received sixty won. We partied on those nights with *sool* and opium.

My boys and I also found work guarding some of the merchants' things. At night, we sold women to these same merchants.

Truth: I had no clue how old I was anymore. I felt like an old man, though. I had forgotten my real name because I hadn't used it in so long. As back in Orang, I slipped into darkness. There was nothing left inside me but a big hole waiting for the *yu-ryeong* to fill, since, as in other markets, I couldn't find ice.

With my brothers, we became men. "You are the man! You are the real man," we would even tell one another. We did grow into men on those streets, and not very nice men.

Sometime that fall of 2001, we headed to the mountain to pick mushrooms. We met up with some peasants who lived in the caves.

They prayed, as my mother had, to the stones and the trees, believing in the power of *shan-shin-ryong-nim* to grant them their wishes, which were usually for more food, to get their houses back, to find their missing sons and daughters, and an end to their poverty. Most blamed the Americans, who were still trying to invade us. Chulho and I would shake our heads while listening to these folk stories. Some of the peasants talked as if Kim Il-sung were still alive and fighting the greatest battle of his life.

"He's a god," said a grandmother living in a mud hut she said she had made herself. "His very spirit is guiding my son, who's in the military, to kick the Americans back once and for all."

"When was the last time you heard from your son?" I asked.

"Two years ago," she said with sparkles in her eyes. "He's doing great work, my son, my *adeul*."

I started laughing so hard I fell to my knees and rolled around on the ground holding my aching stomach. I knew this woman's son was dead, either from fighting or from famine. But she still clung to the legend of Kim Il-sung.

A just death, I thought.

I laughed so hard the woman started to cry, thinking I was some possessed spirit. As Sangchul and Unsik dragged me away, Chulho kicked me hard in the groin. "You're really scaring me," he said. "You've become like a demon."

"Like that guy in Rajin-Seonbong," Unsik added. "You will kill, Chang. Very soon, I know you will."

"Whatever," I said, shaking them loose. "I am what I am!"

"And what is that?" Min-gook asked, stepping toward me. It was the first time in all our years on the street that he got in my face. His arms were crossed, and he was staring me down. I stepped toward him, pounding my fist into the palm of my hand.

"Wanna fight . . . Wanna make it *your* death?" I snapped back at him.

He shook his head and spat.

"You've become a ghost, Chang," Chulho chortled. "Go cool off in the river. Don't come back until you're part of this group again."

Needless to say, I did cool off, or warm up. I needed my brothers, and they needed me, too.

27

I n February 2002 we made up our minds to leave Gyeong-
seong again at the start of planting season. Back to the
coast, maybe—mackerel, dreams of being a shipmate, I
didn't care. Anywhere but Gyeong-seong. All I knew for
certain was that there was nothing left for us in this dead
town.

I was in the train station near the end of February, having just
stolen some twisted bread sticks from the market, when an old
man with bushy salt-and-pepper eyebrows looked right at me and
pointed.

"Come here, boy," he said in a strong, gruff voice.

I sized him up and down before moving toward him. He wore
pressed pants the color of the sea on a winter's day and a matching cotton shirt and cap. I hadn't seen clean clothes on anyone
since we left Pyongyang. His cheeks were not sunken and hallow,
either. He was full and glowing from the winter wind. There was

something about him I recognized. Something about him felt familiar. Yet I couldn't quite make out what.

I pushed the feeling away. *This is a rich man*, I thought, instead, slinking up beside him. I held my hands up, cupped together in front of me, and tilted my head, hoping to look innocent and desperate.

He shook his head. "I don't want to give you handouts," he said. "What is your name?"

I was startled. His accent was from Pyongyang.

I glanced at the poster beside him. On it, in the neat handwriting of an educated man, he had listed the Chinese medicines he was selling: elm tree powder for stomachache, *woo-wong* for the liver, and dried *omija* for bronchial problems. The poster also said the man could make medicines upon order to cure headaches and menstrual cramps.

"You a doctor?" I asked, letting my hands fall to my sides.

"I am," the man replied. "But I asked you a question. What is your name?"

"*Chang*," I said, puffing out my chest and holding my head high. "I'm very fast and accurate at throwing metal chopsticks." I wanted this old man to be scared of me like everyone else. "Want me to work for you, guard your things?"

"What is your real name?" he said, seemingly unimpressed with my attempted bravado or my invitation to work for him.

I shook my head and turned away from him. I refused to answer. If he wasn't going to give me food, won, or a job, he was useless.

"Is your mother Jeongwha?" he asked. "Is your father Seong-il?"

I turned back around and stared at him. His brown, almost amber, pupils drew me toward him. He reminded me of something . . . an animal perhaps. Yes, he had the eyes of a brown bear. No . . . the eyes of a person, someone I knew.

"What?" I finally said. My arms began to tingle, and my face became flushed. "You're a fortune-teller," I spat. "The last seer I met told me death was around me, and it was. My best friend in the entire world, my brother, died."

"What is your real name?" he continued, ignoring me. "Is it Sungju?"

I stared at him for a long time. "Only people who see the dead would know these names," I finally said.

"You're Sungju from Pyongyang, and your mother is Jeongwha. Your father is Seong-il."

"Only those who speak with the dead know these names," I repeated.

"I'm your grandfather," he then said, taking a step toward me.

"No!" I said, stepping back from him.

"Come with me to my home," he continued, folding up his poster and placing some glass jars into a large backpack.

"You're a sorcerer—I can't trust you," I said, flicking my fingers in my nervousness. I wanted to hit this man, to beat him up, to tell him to go away. How dare he say those names to me.

He stopped what he was doing and stared at me, his face soft.

Unsik, Sangchul, Min-gook, and Chulho sauntered over, having taken my flicking fingers as a sign that we were about to engage in battle.

"I'll be back in a minute," I told the old man as I pulled my brothers into a huddle.

"Let's go with him," Unsik said after I explained what was going on. "Steal his things. He's wealthy! Look at his clothes."

"Yes," I said, rubbing my hands together. My initial fear had turned to greed. This man was using me for something. Instead, I would use him.

THE LIGHT ON THE FRONT OF THE OLD MAN'S BIKE DANCED across the snow as we made our way from the train station, through the main town square, and past the monument in honor of Kim Il-sung, with red lettering that said the great leader is with us forever. While there was a nearly full moon hanging low in the sky, clouds kept drifting over it like waves in the sea.

I listened to my shoes crushing the ice, the howl of a dog, and the hum of the motor that generated the old man's light.

"What are your friends' names?" he asked me.

"None of your business," I snapped.

"That's a funny name," he replied.

"How much longer?" I asked after we had walked for what seemed like a few hours, the snow-covered fields replaced by the sloping hills and forests of the countryside. The few wooden houses we passed were in complete darkness.

"About another hour," he replied. "It's quicker on the bike. But I can't take you all. Do you—"

I grunted to cut him off. "Don't ask me any more questions," I hissed.

WE FINALLY TURNED INTO A DRIVEWAY THAT LED TO A house at the foot of a tall mountain. Kerosene lamps had been placed in the windowsills, casting light out into the courtyard.

I followed the old man as he moved toward the house as my brothers tailed behind me. All the while, I surveyed the scene. There was a shed that clearly housed goats. I snapped my fingers on my right hand three times, indicating to my brothers to steal the goats. Then I spied the chicken coop. I snapped my fingers again to indicate that the chickens had to be taken, too. Then I saw the rabbit cages. We would be feasting for months! I thought.

Just as the old man reached up to turn the doorknob, the door opened. A woman stepped outside. She squinted as her eyes got used to the dim light, and I watched as her expression moved from joy to shock when her eyes landed on me. Wearing only socks, she stepped into the snow and headed straight for me.

"*Yaeya*, we've finally found you! You're alive," she said, reaching me and embracing me in her warm arms. My heart started to race.

"No, I am not your grandson," I replied through clenched teeth. This woman was crazy, just like the girl who told me dragons would fall.

"What kind of game are you two playing?" I demanded, pushing the old woman away.

"Come inside," the old woman said in a kind voice. "We'll talk there." She wore her gray hair in a tight bun and a rabbit fur collar over her sweater. She took my hand and pulled me into the house, which smelled of burning cedar.

"I'll get you and your friends some hot water and honey," she said, leaving me standing in the doorway. I looked around at the bookshelves as the old man pushed his way past me. There was one full of Chinese medicines in glass jars and another with leather-bound books. My gaze moved to the kitchen, the open shelves of which were well stocked with rice, noodles, chopsticks, dishes, and spoons. I saw a few chests in the corner of the main room. *So much to steal*, I thought.

Then my eyes landed on a portrait hanging on the opposite wall.

I stopped breathing.

Without taking off my shoes, I inched my way into the center of the room, as if learning to walk.

As I neared the picture, my legs shook, and I tried to breathe, but I couldn't. My chest had become tight, as if a fist had just hit me hard. I felt dizzy and had to reach out to steady myself against the wall. "Am I dreaming?" I asked out loud. No one answered, but I could feel the old man move right in behind me.

I pinched my legs. "Am I awake? Am I dead now? Is this what happens on the other side?"

"You are awake," he whispered. "You're not dead."

I stared at the portrait, first into the eyes of my mother, and then at my father. The black-and-white photograph had been taken on their wedding day. It was a copy of the photograph I had wanted from my mother's wedding chest.

I managed to whistle to let my brothers know to abort our plans. Unsik came rushing in the front door wanting to know what was going on. I whistled again, and he ran outside to get the others.

I then turned on legs that felt like rubber and faced the old man, the old woman, and soon my brothers, all staring at me wide-eyed with mouths agape.

I opened my own mouth to speak. But before any words came, my knees gave out, and I collapsed to the floor.

"What is it?" Min-gook asked, coming to my side.

"This man is my grandfather," I said, my voice faint and weak. "And this woman . . . is my grandmother."

She had fallen to the floor, too, and was sobbing. And my

grandfather—the man who had told me that before every storm is a calm, who lay with me in Bo-Cho's house and told me the story of Heungbu wa Nolbu—smiled.

"You may have grown since I last saw you. You are not a little boy anymore. You're sixteen. I would never forget your face. Every Sunday, I went looking for you," he said as he slid down beside me on the floor. "With every falling star I saw, I knew I was getting closer."

MY BROTHERS AND I TOOK OFF OUR SHOES AND SAT IN A circle around my grandfather as my grandmother finished making us hot water with honey.

"I wrote your mother every week in Pyongyang," he began to explain. "I got worried when she stopped replying. And so I came to look for you. You weren't there. Another family with a little girl about your age lived in your apartment. I asked the block party head where you had all gone. I had to bribe him, but he eventually told me you had moved to Gyeong-seong. I paid him a lot of money for the address, and for nearly a year he refused to give it to me. Finally, he did. But when we got here, it was too late. The people who had taken over your house said your father had disappeared, that your mother had gone to look for food and she had never come back. The man who owned the house said you were a *kotjebi* at the train station and had never come back."

"But I *did* go back to the house," I exclaimed. I couldn't believe what I was hearing. "If the man who had taken over our house had just said, had just told me, that my grandfather—someone—was looking for me, the past four and a half years wouldn't have happened."

"I never gave up hope I would find you," my grandfather said.

"Hope," I whispered. Something I had lost.

"Is this your gang?" my grandmother asked as she shuffled into the room, carrying a clay pot of steaming water.

I nodded.

My grandfather rolled a cigarette while my grandmother poured each of us a cup of hot water and then spooned in honey.

"I have honeybees now," my grandfather said as I took a sip of the drink. Then he quickly asked, "Where is your mother?"

I could tell by his creaky voice that he wanted to know, and yet, at the same time, he was not ready for the answer.

I shook my head slowly. "She went to Wonsan to get food from Aunt Nampo," I said after a long pause. "She never came back. I don't know where she is."

My grandmother spilled part of her drink on her sweater.

"Aunt never mentioned that your mother was ever expected there," my grandfather said, his voice full of tears.

It came to me then what was so familiar about my grandfather's eyes. They drooped in the corners the same way my mother's did.

28

y grandfather slaughtered his best goat to celebrate my being found. "You need to know that even before the famine, killing a goat was done only on special occasions and showed the highest respect for those it was being cooked for and served to."

With the famine, of course, few people had livestock anymore. I had heard stories over the years at the markets of the military killing entire families just to take their pigs and sheep. The military was hungry, too, you know. That my grandfather slaughtered a goat for my brothers and me . . . that gesture alone made me at least feel human again.

We were no longer wild animals who stole, who found customers for nightflowers, who fought, who had become so hardened we forgot our real names. Needless to say, I wondered how my grandfather had so much livestock up here, in the hills, deep in the countryside, miles away from any other home. It was as if his home was that lake in Baekdu Mountain: placed there from heaven.

My brothers and I spent much of the second day vomiting because we were not used to eating so much meat. Our diets had been mostly breads and rice, after all, and lots of insects and bugs and worms that came attached to the food. But being sick didn't stop us. Since we didn't want to appear disrespectful to my grandfather by not eating, we'd throw up and then eat another dish. Vomit again, then eat some more, feasting on the tender goat that was roasted on an outdoor spit and served in bowls with baked radish and potatoes. We boys grew lazy, smoking cigarettes with my grandfather, drinking *sool*, sleeping, and eating. As we relaxed, we recounted many of our journeys, including the gangs we defeated and the brothers we lost.

"Myeongchul was the best actor in Joseon," Chulho told my grandfather.

"And Young-bum was the most loyal of any brothers," I whispered. "He saved me after *abeoji* and *eomeoni* left."

My grandmother stopped listening early on. "I hate hearing how you suffered," she told me as she busied herself in the kitchen, cutting more vegetables. She wanted to give us an endless stream of food for all the meals we'd missed over the years. A tear dripped down my cheek then. She really did love me. Someone, somewhere, was listening to my prayers. Someone, somewhere, still had hope when all of mine had gone.

MY BROTHERS TOLD ME THEY WERE LEAVING ON THE MORN-
ing of the sixth day. They first said it was because they didn't
want to see my grandparents with no food. All of us had managed
to finish off the goat, and my grandfather was about to kill two
chickens and a rabbit for us. But I didn't believe this was the reason.

"We want to live in the train station," Chulho said, pulling
me outside so my grandparents couldn't hear. "The merchants
in Gyeong-seong are paying us to protect their goods. We have
nothing to do here, and soon everyone will go hungry if we keep
eating the way we are. In Gyeong-seong, we have work and food."

"My grandfather has lots of food," I said.

"We want to go," Sangchul cut in.

"Maybe you can come back and forth?" I asked, my voice
sounding desperate. I didn't want to lose them, but I also knew I
wasn't going back to street life, either.

Sangchul placed a warm hand on my shoulder. "We'll miss you,
too—so much you don't even know," he said. "But it's two hours
each way from here to Gyeong-seong. We'll die of exhaustion if
we try that every day. We need to live in the train station."

"It's all we know," Min-gook added. "We want to see if our
families might come looking for us, too. We've only ever kept
moving and looked for them. What if, like with you, we all keep
missing each other?"

"We had a rocky start," Unsik said, stepping toward me. "But . . ."

"But you'll always be my brother," I said, finishing his sentence.

"The best brother I could have," he said with a smile.

"Can you make us a promise?" Chulho said, moving in close.

"Of course, anything," I replied, wiping my eyes.

"Can you come to the train station every Sunday to see us, as your grandfather did looking for you?"

"Yes. Of course."

I then watched my four brothers walk side by side down the road, wearing clothes that my grandmother had washed and sewn. I choked back my tears and swallowed the hurt and sadness swelling inside me. Even before they disappeared from my view, I missed them. I felt hollow all over again, like when my parents left.

FOR THE LAST MONTHS OF WINTER I HELPED MY GRAND-father make his medicines, grinding herbs into fine powders with a wooden pestle-and-mortar hand grinder he had made himself. He taught me the exact amounts of powder to mix with honey or sticky rice powder. I also boiled his syringes and cleaned his glass jars.

A few times every day, someone would pop in: an aging grandmother, a sick child. In one of the many sheds, which he had built himself, he would see the patient, never turning anyone away, even if they couldn't pay. He'd administer whatever medicines were needed, and I'd help him bandage wounds and set broken bones. His patients often gave him food—an animal or vegetables. The men would come by on another day and fix a fence or replace a beam in the chicken coop. Unlike the doctors I'd heard about in Gyeong-seong, my grandfather always gave his medicines to the people along with treatment.

When spring came, I helped my grandfather till the land of the small farm he ran. My hands became calloused from the friction of heaving the shovel up and down. But the land was fertile, and soon I saw the stalks of corn and the soybeans and potatoes pop forth from the ground.

After that, I became a shepherd. Several days a week, I'd take my grandfather's goats to the hills. I'd sing, "'The roll of thunder of Jong-Il peak,'" trying as hard as I could to sound like Sangchul when he performed in the train station. When I was bored of singing, I'd recite myths, including the one of Heungbu wa Nolbu.

Being a shepherd meant having a lot of time to myself; so when my voice grew hoarse from singing and I'd recited the few myths I knew, I'd point my long staff at one of those little creatures in my charge and name it. "You are so much like Min-gook," I said to the beefiest buck. "And you, lean and mean billy, you are Chulho." Half laughing, half crying, I'd then recount to these animals stories of my brothers and what we did together, leaving in the parts I'd left out for my grandfather, including my using opium, kicking other boys when they had already surrendered, and finding men to have sex with the nightflowers.

Since the area where my grandparents lived was deep in the countryside, I could see more stars than I ever had anywhere else. When spring finally moved over to let summer in, I'd lie on the flat roof of one of my grandfather's sheds and stare up at the sky.

One night, my grandfather asked if he could join me. We lay side by side, our hands behind our heads, and stared at Ursa Major. I wanted to tell him the story of Chilseong and her goddess children, but as before when I thought I wanted to share something, I couldn't. The last time I had been this close to a grown man was when my father told me about Chilseong. That time felt so very far away now. It's funny how, after a time, not just a person's scent but also his or her face leaves our memories. All I had left was his story of Chilseong, and I think I didn't want to give that away, not yet.

"Do you remember when you were little, my telling you that if you make a wish on a falling star, the wish will come true?" my grandfather said, and just in the nick of time. I was about to cry thinking of my father.

"Uh-huh," I replied.

"Make a wish now," he said, pointing to the northern horizon as a star blazed across the sky, fast and faint, like the final fizzle of a firecracker on Parade Day. If I didn't hurry, I'd miss it.

I pinched my eyes shut. "You brought me my grandparents," I

said aloud to Chilseong and *shan-shin-ryong-nim*. "Now I want to find my parents. Please lead them to me."

MY GRANDMOTHER HAD BEEN A HIGH SCHOOL MATH teacher when she married my grandfather. She stopped working in her midforties and ran an after-school program for elite math students—that is, until she and my grandfather left Pyongyang to come looking for my family and me.

One rainy afternoon, I found my grandfather in one of his sheds, nailing planks of wood together, and then those planks onto a flat piece of plywood, creating a box. Then he poured sand into it. "We have no notebooks," he explained as he waved his hands over the contraption. "This," he said with a wide smile, "will be how you study at the house of your grandmother."

After I did household chores or in the evenings on those days I had to shepherd, my grandmother would take me to that shed. For hours, she had me doing math equations and writing paragraphs in the sand.

I soon slipped back into study mode, replacing my need for cigarettes and *sool* with words and algebra. In the hills, while tending the goats, I'd use my walking stick and continue my studies on my own in the dusty earth.

At night I'd fall asleep in down bedding and wake up to my grandfather's snores filling the house and my grandmother's porridge cooking over slow heat on the stove. I could exhale and relax and sleep so deeply I wondered if I had slept at all in the past four years. On some days that hole inside me was filled, and time didn't seem to move.

On other days, though, I'd wake to the sound of a magpie cawing or the call of the rooster, panting, not quite sure where I was, patting the bedding down and calling for my mother. My grandfather would calm me by stroking my back and then giving me hot water with honey. As he rocked me in his arms, he sang:

> "Hushabye, hushabye baby
> sleep well
> go to a country of dream
> my lovely baby
> go to a country of dream
> my lovely baby."

EVERY SUNDAY, THE MOMENT THE ROOSTER ANNOUNCED dawn, I'd jump into my pants and sweater and head out the front door with the big gray canvas bag full of food my grandmother packed the night before. I'd race, more times than not running the entire way to Gyeong-seong, to the train station to see my brothers. By the time I got there, I'd be perspiring, and my feet would be blistered. But I ignored my discomfort. I had discovered I had two homes, you see, two places that drew me to them, as metal does a magnet. My grandparents and my brothers.

On hot, humid days when the cicadas hummed and the crickets sang, my brothers and I went to Gyeong-seong River to swim. We'd swing on an old tire tied to a tree on a fraying rope and leap off into the stream. We'd play tag, too, during which we would chase one another, splashing and singing at the top of our lungs.

We'd end our days by my buying them twisted bread sticks in the market using won my grandfather gave me from selling his medicines. We'd sit on the broken stone steps leading up to the train station and stare at the sunset. One time, I thought about Pyongyang and wondered why I was ever in such awe of our capital city, why everyone held it in such great esteem. I came to realize then and there that gilded castles in the sky aren't ever buildings. They're people. My gilded castle was here, all along, with my friends, my brothers, Chulho, Min-gook, Sangchul, Unsik, Myeongchul, and Young-bum.

Inside, we already know the things that will happen to us in life. We spend our days just waiting for them to be revealed . . . I remembered my grandfather's words then. I guess as a child, when I played with my toy soldiers under the baby grand piano and wished for a sibling, I had known I had some, somewhere out there. I was just waiting for time to reveal them to me.

I guess, also, I always knew that I'd have to leave my brothers for good . . . at least in body.

In spirit, my brothers and I would always be one.

29

On a late fall day, when the air outside was crisp and smelled of my grandmother's cooking fires and damp leaves and the wind bit into my cheeks as I walked with the goats, I arrived home in the evening to find my grandfather pacing the driveway.

When he saw me, he motioned for me to leave the goats and follow him. His face was drawn. I could tell, even in the dim light, that he was tense.

In his examination room, which smelled of disinfectant, a man was seated in the old wooden chair where my grandfather usually sat. The man seemed nervous as he folded his gray cotton cap into his hands and stood up. "You must be Sungju!"

I stared into his black eyes and nodded slowly.

"He says he knows your father," my *hal-abeoji* said, gesturing for me to sit on the patient's cot.

I turned to my grandfather and tilted my head, unsure I had heard correctly.

"He says he has been sent by your father, who is living in China," my grandfather continued. "The man wants to give you something."

My hands trembled as I carefully opened the letter the man passed to me.

> *Dear darling son,*
>
> *I'm living in China very safely. Please come to China to see me. This man will take you. I have looked a long time for you.*
>
> *My love,*
>
> *Father*

My eyes filled with tears, from relief that my father had found me but also from anger.

My mother was missing.

I had spent four years stealing, begging, and living on the streets. And he'd been in China the entire time? He finally sent me a letter addressed "Dear darling son," as if the years had not grown like a sea separating us?

I wanted to scream. I fought the impulse to tear up the letter. *Who cares where he is?* I wanted to lash out.

Instead, I started to pass the letter back to the man, my hands shaking more than ever, when I saw that my father had written more on the back.

> In case you do not believe this letter is from me
> . . . When you were little, we used to picnic on the
> banks of the Daedong River. Afterward, we played
> war games. I taught you military tactics, remember?
> One of those tactics was to have a secret code. If we
> ever got separated in battle, we would use that code
> to identify each other. One of us would have to start
> the code, the other had to answer it. I will start: the
> Korean consonant N.

The tears came crashing down my cheeks. It was the start of the code, what my father was supposed to say or write, to identify himself. I leaned over, unable to breathe. For a moment I couldn't see, blinded by my crying. I knew this was my father. In our secret code game, father would give me a random consonant, and I had to answer with a word that began with that consonant.

The man finally spoke. "I'm a friend of your father's." I didn't look up, and I started to shake. "I will take you to him," he continued. I wished I hadn't heard that. I didn't want to.

Fury, love, hurt, and guilt had all rolled themselves into one tight ball that got stuck in my stomach and threatened to choke me.

"Give the boy time to think," my grandfather said, I guess sensing something wasn't right with me. "Come back in two days' time. We'll have a decision by then."

ALL THAT NIGHT, I TOSSED AND TURNED, TRYING TO SLEEP but waking at the faintest of sounds, including a twig falling on the roof, the rustling of leaves from the wind. *Tomorrow I will tend the goats. Tomorrow will be a normal day, like any other*, I'd tell myself. *Tomorrow I will forget completely about this strange man's visit.*

But then my mind would drift to that letter. *I'm living in China very safely. Please come to China to see me. This man will take you. I have looked a long time for you. My love, Father.*

I wanted to see my father—that much I came to realize. But not to run into his arms and hug him. Instead, to ask him why he left and never came home. "Why, why didn't you honor your promise and return in a week? *Eomeoni* once told me that you could brave anything except the thought of my thinking of you as a failure, too."

"I WILL GO WITH THE MAN," I TOLD MY GRANDPARENTS THE next morning as we sipped hot water with honey and I ran a spoon through a bowl of porridge.

"What if it's a trap?" my grandmother whispered. "What if this man doesn't know your father and wants to hurt you?"

I explained to her that in the letter something was written that no one else in the world but my father would ever know. "At least the letter is real. It's my father's handwriting. He used our secret code."

My grandfather cleared his throat. "I, too, am worried about you going to China. I don't trust this man. For four years we have not heard a thing from either your mother or father, and now—"

"I'm coming back," I said, cutting him off, reaching over and taking first my grandmother's and then my grandfather's hands in my own. "I want to live here and grow old with you."

My grandmother gasped, and my grandfather sighed and lowered his head. "We want that, too, but . . ."

"But what? I thought this is what you wanted. I thought this was the reason you came looking for me."

"There is no hope for Joseon," my grandfather said, looking up, his eyes a pool of tears. "If you can get out—I mean, out of Joseon—you should go. I just . . . I just . . . I just want to make sure this is the right way with this stranger."

Now I was really confused. The Chinese hunt us down like rats, wanting to exterminate us, and the South gets information from us, then kills us. "Where is there to go?" I finally said.

My grandfather shrugged.

I pressed on, trying to be as reassuring as I possibly could be. "Look, this isn't a trap. This man has a letter from my father. That much I know for certain. I survived four years in train stations and back alleys. I can survive this."

MY GRANDMOTHER SLIPPED A BAG WITH RICE BALLS AND honey over my shoulder. My grandfather, whom I knew well by now, chain-smoked when he was nervous, and he lit up one after another of his hand-rolled cigarettes as we waited for the stranger to return to take me to China.

When the man, who looked as though he was in his early thirties and who reminded me of Chulho, arrived, he reassured my grandparents that we could trust him.

I didn't cry as we walked down the road or look back after I had bowed to my grandparents, even though I could hear my grandmother sobbing at the doorway. I had to fight every nerve in my body that wanted me to turn around and run back into her arms.

And then they were gone. All I could hear was my feet crunching the snow underneath me.

"Why didn't my father come sooner?" I asked the man.

"He tried. He sent people to look for you and your mother." His speech was curt. I got the sense he really didn't want to talk.

"Why didn't he come back?" I pressed on.

"We're all in hard times, even those in China," the man began. He was thin, but I could tell by his strong gait that he was fit. I was breathing heavily to keep up. *This man has walked many mountains,* I thought. *He's well trained.*

"What does that mean?" I asked. "My father couldn't come home? He got stuck in China for four years?"

The man stopped and spun me around so I had to look at him.

"The less you know, the better," he said sternly. "Just trust this: Every arrangement possible has been made to ensure your security. Your father has done a lot to find you and bring you to him and avoid being caught."

"By the border guards?" I asked. The man was walking again and grunted. I reached out to him and held his elbow, getting him to stop again.

"Can I at least say goodbye to my brothers in Gyeong-seong before we leave?" I asked him. We studied each other's faces. I was looking particularly into his eyes to see signs of deceit. There were none. He was a hard man, for sure, but I felt he could be trusted.

"Yes, you can see your brothers," he finally whispered, shifting from one shoulder to the other the bag of food my grandmother had given him, saying it was for the boys. "But you need to listen to me at all times. If I say jump, you ask how high. This is one of the most dangerous journeys in the world you are about to take. You're a street boy, so you know people, whom to trust and whom not to trust. You know danger. You also know how to act calm in the face of danger. That's why I know we'll be okay. But stop asking questions. That's your first order."

"What's your name?" I asked as he huffed off.

"None of your business," he called over his shoulder.

I smiled then.

He reminded me of . . . well, me.

MY BROTHERS WEREN'T ANYWHERE AT THE GYEONG-SEONG train station. The man started to get impatient as I searched for them, snapping at me at one point that I couldn't waste any more time. We had to go.

"You seem to know what it's like as a street boy," I said. He glared at me, but I didn't care. "Everyone in these boys' lives has let them down. Everyone. And you know that. So I'm not leaving until I find them. You can leave if you want, but I'm staying."

The man sighed, stepped back, and said he'd wait for me by the willow tree by Ha-myeon Bridge. It was the same tree where Chulho and Min-gook sat that late-summer day in 1997 when I sold my textbooks.

I finally found my brothers in the market. I waved them over and gave them my grandmother's food.

"But it's not Sunday," Chulho said, tilting his head and eyeing me up and down. "Something up? Everything okay with the grandfolks?"

"Yeah," I replied slowly. "I have to go to Hweryeong. My mother's sister, Nampo, now lives there. She's ill." I felt sick inside from the first and what would become the last lie I ever told them. I wanted to take it back, swallow it, and start all over. Tell them the truth.

Then I reminded myself that what I was about to do with this strange man was illegal and considered treason by the government.

"We'll come with you," said Sangchul, tossing his bag over his shoulder.

The others nodded.

"No," I said, shaking my head. "I have to go on my own. But I will try to be back, if not this Sunday, the Sunday after. Soon . . . very soon."

"Okay . . . ," said Chulho.

I could tell by the way he looked at me that he knew I was lying. But then his eyes moved to a woman carrying a basket of boiled eggs a little too loosely in front of her, as though she was new to selling and unprepared to face *kotjebi*.

Min-gook, Sangchul, Unsik, and Chulho all grunted goodbye to me and were then gone in a flash, following the woman.

"If not this Sunday, then the one after I will come and see you," I whispered as they disappeared into the crowd. "A promise is a promise. And I mean that. Whatever I face in China, whatever man my father has become, I will be back here in a week to see you and live with my grandparents again."

THE STRANGE MAN PAID AN OLD TRUCK DRIVER, WHO looked as beat-up as his vehicle, to let us hitch a ride in the back.

We got off the truck around midnight in Hweryeong. "We'll

stay here at a friend's house," the man said. And I mean that's all he said. This stranger had gone mute on me.

I spent the rest of that night and all of the next day inside this so-called friend's house. I was unable to eat my grandmother's rice balls, unable to sleep, unable to do much but stare out at nothing and think about all the things I wanted to tell my father, every detail of my life over the past four years that he was responsible for. At least my anger toward my father, I thought at one point, made me not think about what I was about to do: Smuggle myself into China. I should have been way more worried about that than I actually was.

Toward midnight, the man and I were on our way again. There was no moon, and it was cloudy, which the man said he was happy about. "So no one can see us," he said. At least he was talking again.

We met a chain-smoking border guard at the edge of the Duman River on the outskirts of Hweryeong, far from the bridge that connected Joseon with China. The guard spoke fast and in a low voice. "You have to cross the river as quickly as you can," he said as I slipped off my shoes and tied them together. I then draped my shoes around my neck to keep them dry. The stranger handed the guard a wad of won. "Go," the guard said, turning around and walking up the hill.

I waded into the cool water, cooler than the snow I would put on my feverish head in the winter as a child. I held my bag of food from my grandmother over my head as my feet began to slope downward and I slowly sank into the mucky part of the river.

"Follow me," the man ordered, obviously having done this before. I walked right in behind him, my toes gripping the bottom of the river like the talons of ravens grab their prey. The water was low, but the undercurrent was strong. A current, I thought at one point, that could wash me right out to the East Sea.

On the other side of the river, I put my shoes back on, and then, soaking wet, followed the man as he walked at a very fast pace into the woods and then into the hills.

We walked so far, so fast—a steady march; run is the best way to describe it. I was on my own *arduous walk*, but going in the opposite direction than Kim Il-sung had gone as a child. I was going into China, a China full of steep mountains with crags and holes.

At sunrise, the man stopped at the door of a wooden farm shed on top of one of the mountains: a shed like the one in which Myeongchul died. A shed that overlooked a pear and sunflower farm. We went inside, and he told me I could lie down. I did. Within seconds, I fell into a deep sleep.

ake up, *adeul*," I heard my father's voice say. I sat bolt upright, my body shaking from the tremor of having been disturbed deep inside a dream. For a moment I thought I was back in Pyongyang and everything I had lived in the past four and a half years was a dream.

But then I smelled perspiration mixed with greasy, boiling soybean oil and cigarette smoke. I looked around. The shed was lit by a kerosene lamp set to low, and I saw the faces of two men. The stranger who had led me across the river was sitting closer to me than the other man, and his face was lined in stubble and his eyes dark, as if he hadn't slept a wink. He was dressed for outside, wearing his thick wool coat. Night had fallen, I could see that much as my eyes darted toward the small window and then back at the man. I must have slept all day.

The other man, who was older, with gray hair and a round, full face, waved to the table beside me, on top of which was a steamy twisted bread stick, a bowl of rice with pork, and some candies.

"What is this?" I demanded as the men moved the table toward me.

"Food," the man who led me across the river said. "You need to eat to keep your strength up. I'm returning to Joseon," he said matter-of-factly. "This man, who also will not tell you his name, will take you to your father."

All of a sudden I felt sick. "I thought you said you were one of my father's friends?" I was filled with the heavy weight of knowing that this was a trick, just as my grandparents had feared. I had gone along with it because I wanted to believe, deep down, that I was wrong. "You don't know my father at all," I said before the man could reply, my voice weighted with hopelessness.

"No," he said, passing me the steaming twisted bread stick and gesturing for me to eat. "I never met your father. I'm just a delivery person, and I have my own family in Joseon. This is my business, taking people back and forth. I'm what you call a human smuggler. A broker."

"Take me with you," I pleaded.

"No," he replied, a little too quickly. His mind was made up. He was a brick wall.

"Are you taking me to jail?" I turned and asked the other man. "Are you going to hurt me?"

"Shush, boy," the second man said, coming over and stroking

my shoulder. I brushed his hand away. "I really am your father's friend . . . your father's best friend. Your father is in Hangook. I am taking you as far as I can go, and then shortly after that you will meet your father. I promise you can trust me. I know that people have let you down."

"You mean my father has let me down," I snapped, though I did not intend to.

"People have let you down," he repeated. "Trust will be hard. But do try to trust me. If we are to make it to your father, you need to."

"Where is Hangook?" I asked. I wanted to go back to Joseon right then and there. I wanted to hear my grandfather's deep voice and my grandmother's sweet singing when she thought no one was listening.

"It's in Daehanminguk," he answered as he gave the man who had brought me over the river some Chinese yuan. "I need you to change." He passed me a pile of neatly pressed clothes. As he turned up the lamp, I pulled the clothes apart and saw a pair of navy-blue slacks, a light blue cotton shirt, a new wool coat, and a pair of shiny black loafers. As I examined the clothes, the man who had brought me over the river opened the door and shut it quickly, sending a gust of air and a golden leaf around the room. He didn't even say goodbye.

"Why do I need to change?" I asked, pinching my eyes shut, remembering Young-bum and his school uniform.

"Promise not to ask too many questions," the man said with a smile.

The man brought me a bucket of water and then helped me wash my hair. After I cleaned the dirt from the crossing from my face and body, I changed into the new clothes.

The man then took a photograph of me. A flash on the camera nearly blinded me.

"What's that for?" I asked as he tucked the camera into a bag. "Jail?" Maybe I was in prison now.

"Remember, knowing less is more in this case," he replied, smiling again. He was a heavier man, with soft eyes that danced in the light from the lamp. Any other time he might really be one of my father's friends, I thought watching him. I might even trust him.

"Just go along with everything I say, and you will be safe," he repeated.

THE MAN MADE ME STAY IN THE SHED FOR NEARLY A WEEK, where I was left alone during the days. I wasn't allowed to go outside, light one of the lamps, or peer out the window. At night, the man would come and sleep beside me on a mat. I did have plenty of blankets and meals, delicious meals, of noodles and pork, tofu and seaweed, even moon cakes.

On the morning of the eighth day, or rather before dawn on the eighth day, the man and I traveled by foot down the mountain and then along dirt paths and on a road to Yanji. "Yanji is in the Yanbian Korean prefecture," he explained, "where many Korean families have lived since before Kim Il-sung, escaping the Japanese."

The Yanji train station was bustling with people, many of whom spoke Korean in dialects my ears strained to understand. As well, I heard a choppy language, which the man whispered to me was Mandarin. In Yanji, there were also cars, trucks, tractors, and motorbikes. The exhaust and all the people made me feel nauseated. I gripped the man's arm tight, fearing I would faint.

In the train station, there was electricity and shining lights all around me, lights I had not seen since Pyongyang, lights that hung low from the ceiling. Many of the people at the train station wore bright colors, too, as they did on parade days in Pyongyang. The women wore tight dresses that revealed every curve of their bodies, in shiny satin materials, in blues, reds, and yellows. I tried to pretend nothing was a surprise to me, that it all was normal. But in truth, my sense of sight was on overload. Everything was overwhelming, and I started to feel as though I was getting a bad headache.

"After we take our seats," the man whispered into my ear as the whistle from an approaching train and the sound of screeching wheels drowned out most other sounds, "just pretend to sleep. I will do all the talking. Keep your eyes shut at all times."

As I sat back in my seat, my head pounded. I heard a ticket taker come up to the man and say something in Mandarin. I heard the ruffling of papers and then the ticket taker's shoes shuffling off.

I didn't open my eyes until the man who claimed to be my father's best friend nudged me. He leaned over and whispered into my ear that we were getting off at the next station. I rubbed my eyes, pretending that I had really slept the entire way. As an announcement in Mandarin came on the loudspeaker, the man slipped a small envelope onto my lap. He whispered again into my ear when the intercom overpowered other noises. "Inside is your passport. It's a book that will help you travel. You show it to the people who ask to see it. We're going to take a taxi to the airport. I will walk you through the airport to your gate. After you get on the airplane, do not say anything, not even a word. If you do, your accent will reveal where you are from, and you will be caught and sent to jail—you will be sent from China to North Korea. As soon as the airplane lands, you can say anything you like. Your father is waiting for you when the plane lands."

I swallowed hard, nodded, and bowed with a smile, as if this man and I had just had a lighthearted conversation.

At the airport, people moved past and around me, not noticing me or seeming to care.

The man and I finally reached a point where he needed a ticket to pass.

He had me take out mine and the little book he said was a passport. He then pushed me toward a woman standing behind a tall desk. I looked down the entire time she examined my pass-port and plane ticket until I heard her say in Korean for me to move on.

I followed the other people, people who I hoped were on my plane, down a bridge and onto a vehicle, a big bus with wings, a large white swan. I'd never been on a plane before. I'd only ever seen airplanes in the sky, in Pyongyang. I found the seat number that matched the number on my ticket. I sat down, clutching to my chest the bag my grandmother had given me, filled with food, including a jar of my grandfather's honey.

"WHERE ARE YOU FROM?" I HEARD AN OLDER FEMALE VOICE say in Korean. I opened my eyes and looked over. She was sitting beside me, looking at me. Middle-aged, I thought. A mother, but a mother wearing bright red lipstick, and her eyes were lined in heavy black pencil. Her hair was long, stretching down her back. I'd never seen a woman wear makeup like this before.

"Where are you from?" she repeated, smiling, revealing straight, perfectly white teeth.

I started waving, remembering not to speak until the plane landed. She furrowed her eyebrows. "You don't talk?" she asked.

I nodded.

"Mute?"

I nodded.

I could understand her Korean, but it was hard. It moved the words up and down, rising at the end, not lilting like a flower past bloom. She passed me a piece of paper and a big fat pencil with a red tip. "Write," she said, "where you are from."

I started to perspire. This was a trap. The woman was the police. I looked over again, and she was smiling at me.

I wrote down the only place I knew in China. The place the man said my father lived: Hangook.

She looked up after reading and smiled.

She then turned away and looked out the window.

I gripped the sides of the seat as the airplane started to move, inching away from the bridge and then moving faster—soon so fast that I felt sick all over again.

I closed my eyes as the wheels left the ground.

For two hours, I felt every movement, the back and forth, as when I floated in the East Sea in Eodaejin.

Then down.

"Welcome to Daehanminguk," a voice said over a loudspeaker.

This time the words were in an even different Korean dialect than what I'd been hearing, one that was more full, robust, the syllables of the words more drawn out. As the plane came to a stop, I remembered what the smuggler had said about my being able to talk as soon as the plane landed. I turned to the woman who had been sitting beside me, smiled, and said hello: "*Annyeonghaseyo.*"

She made a *tsk-tsk* sound with her mouth and said I shouldn't play games. She then pushed her way in front of me as we lined up to get off the plane.

I followed the people into the terminal, staring at all the signs in Korean that lit up the walls, thinking we must still be somewhere near Yanji. I was confused as to why I had to take an airplane if I wasn't really going anywhere. But I brushed the worry aside, reminding myself that my brothers and I took the train just to get from one end of Cheongjin to the other.

In the terminal, I searched every male face for my father's, but I couldn't see him anywhere. I wondered if maybe after all this time I wouldn't recognize him.

I got whisked up in the crowd, which was headed somewhere, so I followed.

I came to a stop at the back of a long line, where people were showing their passports to people behind more tall desks. This time I handed my passport and ticket to a man, slim and tall, whose hair was cut short, his bangs pushed off his face. He was wearing a skinny tie with his button-down shirt. I stifled a laugh. His costume looked funny.

The man opened my passport and looked at the picture and then me.

He then stared into my face, as if studying every line, making me uncomfortable. I blushed and looked down. "I have to meet my father," I eventually said, just wanting to speak to fill the silence between us, to get him to allow me to go.

"You have to come with us," he finally said.

"No, why do I have to go with you? I have to meet my father," I said, looking up.

"Because your passport . . . Sir, you need to come with us."

Two men in black uniforms emerged from a door behind the man and headed straight toward me. I turned and ran, at top speed, like Chulho and Min-gook racing toward the moving freight train.

I saw a door, over which was a lit-up red sign, and ran up to it, hoping it would just open and I could escape. But when my body hit the door, it wouldn't budge. I couldn't find the doorknob. I slapped at the door, hoping somehow it would open, as the two men caught up to me.

I felt their heavy hands on my back. They grabbed my arms, and before I knew it, they had me lying facedown on the floor with my arms behind me and my wrists cuffed together in some metal device from which I could not escape.

"WHERE ARE YOU FROM?" ASKED THE MAN BEHIND A METAL desk in a brightly lit room.

"Joseon," I said in a low voice. I wrung my hands together. They were no longer cuffed but were sore. "Joseon," I repeated.

"You're from the Democratic People's Republic of Korea?" he asked, his face and voice heavy with shock.

I nodded.

"How did you get here?"

"By airplane," I said.

"How did you get on the plane?"

"With that," I said, pointing to my passport that was in front of him.

"Where did you get this passport?" he asked, waving it in the air.

"Well . . . I found it on the street," I lied. I didn't trust this man, that's for sure.

"This passport is fake," he said.

"No, it must not be true. There is my picture in it. See." I opened it and showed the man the photograph that was taken of me in the shed. "I have to meet my father," I pressed on.

"What is your father's name, son?"

"Why do I have to tell you?" I was now afraid. Maybe this was Joseon and I was in prison. Maybe this was my interrogator, prying me for information about my family.

"Do you know where you are now?" he asked.

"Of course. I am in Hangook," I answered with confidence.

"Do you know where Hangook is?"

"Yes, it is in Daehanminguk."

"Do you know what Daehanminguk means?"

"Yes," I replied more slowly, cautiously, trying hard to hide my growing distress. Where was I really? "It's the name of a city in China," I finally said, hoping, so hoping, that this was true.

"No, Daehanminguk is what you would call Namjoseon."

I stopped breathing and found myself slipping off the chair and onto the floor. When I was in North Korea, South Korea was called Namjoseon, not Daehanminguk. When it finally hit me that I was in South Korea, I remembered the stories I'd heard on the street about how police in the South got us to like them, tell them our secrets, and then killed us. I shimmied onto my knees and put my hands up into the air the way I did when I prayed with my mother. Trembling, with saliva now dripping down my chin, I pleaded with the man to send me back to Joseon. "Don't hurt me, just send me home to my grandparents. I am just a child," I begged. "Please do not kill me."

The man got up then and said I was going to be transferred to Daeseong Gongsa, "the investigation center for people from North Korea."

He then departed, leaving me still kneeling.

THE DINNER I HAD THAT NIGHT AT DAESEONG GONGSA WAS the best I'd had since my birthdays in Pyongyang—chicken and pork and many side dishes. But the meal tasted bittersweet, for all I could think about was that this is what police in the South did: Fatten us people from Joseon up, then slaughter us as the Chinese do their dogs.

The next day, another tall Korean man led me to a room with a big desk in it. A man wearing a skinny tie sat on one side. This time, I didn't laugh at his outfit. He had me sit across from him.

He passed me a pad of paper and some pencils and said he wanted me to write down everything I knew about North Korea. "You can draw or write . . . whatever it is you can. A map of your home, your city, the names of your relatives . . ."

I stared at the paper and pencils as the man stared at me, tapping his foot and glancing every now and then at a clock on the wall. At midday, I was given *yukgaejang*, a hot spicy meat stew.

"Please give us anything," the man finally said midafternoon. My pads of paper were still white. I hadn't written or drawn a thing.

"We want to help you," he pressed on. "We're not your enemies."

Exactly what the interrogators in Joseon told prisoners to get them to spill their secrets, I wanted to snap at the man.

I finally wrote that my family was from Gyeong-seong; that my parents and grandparents were poor potato farmers; that I went to school only until grade four; after that, I had to work the fields; and that I was illiterate and unable to write anything more. I lied about everything, even my family name.

After the man looked at the paper, he asked me again to write about Joseon. "Tell me anything, just something truthful this time," he said in a kind voice.

"Lee Seong-il," I finally blurted out my father's name. "My father, the father I was supposed to meet, who is waiting for me somewhere."

"Come with me," the man said, standing up. He was smiling now. *This is it,* I thought, *I am being sent to my death.* I moved on trembling legs, just as the prisoners I'd seen back in Gyeong-seong did before they were executed. I'd said my father's name, and that was enough. Death. Death to me and soon to him, wherever he was.

I collapsed just outside the door, weeping. I didn't want to be hung in the basement or taken to a courtyard and shot.

The man had to carry me under my arms down the corridor, which was lit with long bulbs that made the man's skin look green.

We passed many doors with windows beside them. My eye caught something inside one of the windows. Something made me stand up straight. I pulled myself away from the man. Whatever it was, I felt a magnet pulling me inside.

All I could see was the back of another man.

I didn't need to see his face.

I could tell by his broad shoulders and stocky stance.

My father.

The man who was interrogating me showed me how to push the metal bar to open the door. When I did so, my father turned. I couldn't even say the word *father*, tears and hurt and pain flooded out of me. I did love him, after all. I was never as happy as this to see him.

He ran to me and pulled me tightly into his arms. "Son, *adeul*," he said, sobbing harder than me. We both fell to the floor, like when *eomeoni* and I collapsed the day Kim Il-sung died, and in each other's arms, we rocked back and forth.

Unlike that day when Kim Il-sung died, this time I did wail, harder than I ever had, inhaling my father's musky scent that as a child made me feel safe at night. So many images passed in front of my eyes as we cradled each other: my brothers, my mother, my grandfather, my grandmother, Bo-Cho . . . I was pretty sure, too, I even saw in my mind's eye those floating blue and soft white lights I first saw in the forest. The *shan-shin-ryong-nim.*

"Home," I whispered in my father's ear when we finally stopped crying, "is not a place, but people. I came to realize that as a street boy. You are one of my homes. And this time I am never letting you leave again."

Epilogue

left North Korea at the age of sixteen and have never returned. I can't. As a North Korean defector with South Korean citizenship, I would be considered a traitor by the government of Joseon and would be imprisoned.

Not long after I arrived in South Korea, my father told me
why we were kicked out of Pyongyang, but I cannot write it here.
You see, my father was in the military. He and his story are known
by the regime. Disclosing the reason would identify him and put
the few relatives of my family still in North Korea at risk. I will
say that if he had done what he did in a free country, such as the
United States, his actions would be viewed as merely part of the
democratic process. But in Pyongyang, they resulted in my family's expulsion from the capital city and eventual separation.

When my father left Gyeong-seong in the winter of 1998
for China, he did become trapped, as my brothers and I on the
street speculated. Our Gyeong-seong neighbors didn't have

border guards working for them, contrary to what they told my father. Trafficking people and goods—going back and forth between North Korea and China—was, and still is, very dangerous. Had my father done so, it might have been his execution that the schoolchildren watched.

My father met a human smuggler in China who said the best thing for him to do was to go to South Korea and then send for my mother and me. South Korea recognizes North Koreans as citizens, and despite rumors I had heard in North Korea, South Korea does not kill defectors. My father thought South Korea would be the safest place for us. Believing that the journey from China to South Korea would be just a few weeks, my father agreed. Unlike my journey, which my father paid a small fortune to orchestrate, my father's exodus from North Korea to South Korea took six months. When he finally arrived in South Korea, it took another year for him to settle. By the time he was able to afford to send a smuggler back to find us, my mother and I had both left Gyeong-seong.

My father, like my grandfather, never gave up hope that he would find us. For four years he used all his income to pay for people to look for my mother and me. To this day, he still pays human smugglers in China and North Korea to search for my mother, whom we have never found. In fact, no one has even been able to find a shred of evidence as to where she went when she left Gyeong-seong.

I didn't integrate well in South Korea, at least not at first. I was angry all the time. I had lost my childhood on the streets, and all I knew how to do was fight. South Korean children were not kind to me, viewing all North Koreans as their poorer and less respected cousins. I had been in South Korea for a year and a half and going to a Presbyterian church every Sunday with my father. I didn't really like it. I didn't understand Jesus at that time, and I felt the hierarchy and rules of the church were too similar to North Korea's. But after a rich South Korean boy, the school bully, egged me on in a fight and I won, and the principal of my school threatened to have me expelled, I went to the church. It was a weekday, and I skulked around the outside. The pastor was clearing the garden. He saw me and asked what I was doing. I told him I wanted to study. I wanted his help. He took me inside his church and gave me a sheet of paper and a pencil.

"Write why you want to study," he told me. "Then I'll think about helping you."

Being a street boy, I had learned how to lie to get what I wanted from merchants. So I wrote a long, flowery essay about how I wanted to be a judge in his society. I wanted to protect justice. I wrote a beautiful dream about how I wanted to protect defectors from North Korea, because even though they have a good place to live in South Korea, they have difficulty in school and landing a job because of prejudice against them. Someone has to protect them from injustice, and that person would be me.

But as I was nearing the end, I looked up, and my eye caught some dust floating in a beam of light streaming in from a stained-glass window. I remembered Gyeong-seong then, and I suddenly thought: *This essay is not from my heart.* (At least not then. Yes, it did become my dream, but I didn't know it at that time.) I put the pencil down and remembered something my mother told me while she prayed over her bowl of water: *If you truly, truly want something, you have to be honest. That's what the water represents in my bowl. Try to empty your mind. Clean it of impure thoughts. Be honest and tell the truth.*

"I just want to study," I wrote the pastor. And that's all I wrote.

The pastor asked not to be named in this epilogue because he does not want praise for what he did after he read these words. It was all part of his selflessness, a selfless path of service that he eventually taught me. The pastor has two daughters and one son. His second daughter was supposed to go to the United States to study. She deferred a semester to teach me. As my tutor, she helped me pass my middle-school examinations so I could go to high school. In high school, I graduated high in my class—Oh, and after my fight with the rich school bully, I never fought again . . . ever.

On my entrance interview for the university, my professor asked me two questions, the second of which was: How can we prepare for the reunification of the two Koreas?

"How we are to reunify keeps changing," I told him. "As a result, so many youngsters have no interest in reunification. They don't know what to believe. But reunification is coming, so we have to prepare. We have nearly thirty thousand North Korean defectors in South Korea. We have to work with them, not isolate them. If we cannot be their friends, we cannot prepare for unification. The key, then, is in South Korea. First step: Unite all the Koreans within South Korea. Get rid of this mentality that South Koreans are superior and North Koreans are inferior. This cannot solve any problems. Approach each other as friends and learn."

For a while in my freshman year, studying political science and journalism at Sogang University, I began to struggle with my studies. My grades were poor. I lost focus of my dream of friendship and reunification. I lost hope I could make my dreams a reality. I was depressed with all the work. I was anxious and overwhelmed. I felt for a while that studying was a waste of time: studying and taking exams, studying and taking more exams. I found the process very boring. But I had learned a valuable lesson as a street boy: "You can't wait for hope to find you. You have to go out and grab it."

By the end of my freshman year, I began to get involved in public-speaking contests and I gave speeches. If I participated, I felt I could learn from others in these debates and meet people with similar dreams, who could inspire me. By the start of my sophomore year in 2011, my hope had returned to help in the reunification of the two Koreas. I realized that to achieve my dream, I had to study and find some way to enjoy studying. I knew, after everything I'd been through and how far I had come, I couldn't drop out. I learned how to deal with the stress, and soon I came to love school. The more I study, the more I see what I don't know and want to learn.

I grew up being brainwashed that America was evil. As a result, I didn't trust Caucasians. In 2010, though, I was given the opportunity to study English at Arizona State University. At first, I was worried to go, because America was my sworn enemy. Yet I went. I saw that Caucasians don't have horns on their heads. I now have so many American friends. I feel the only thing different about us is our skin color. Oh, and our politics. Real freedom to me is democracy, in which you can do what you want, but you also have to take responsibility for yourself. I came to understand in America that this is what I never had. I feel the first sixteen years of my life were stolen from me. Stolen by the government of North Korea, and that's why I study so hard, to make up for all the lost time.

In October 2015, I started my master's degree in international relations at the University of Warwick in England on a Chevening scholarship, which is funded by the UK government. I was also accepted to the London School of Economics.

After my master's degree, I hope to pursue a doctorate in the same area. While there are many experts on Korean reunification, there are few who are from North Korea. Yet our voices are needed. To help gain diplomatic experience, I interned in 2014 with Canadian member of Parliament Barry Devolin as part of a program funded by HanVoice, a North Korean advocacy organization. In the late summer and fall of 2015, I worked for the UK Embassy in Seoul, South Korea.

MY INTEREST IN THE HUMAN RIGHTS OF DEFECTORS CAME by way of personal experience. My father and I have never given up looking for my mother. In 2009, a smuggler gave us a lead of a woman living in China who was very similar to my mother in both appearance and background. My father and I went to China to meet her.

It wasn't my mother.

My father and I were silent in the taxi on the way back to the airport until, as we were pulling into the departure zone, my father turned to me and said, "*Adeul,* that woman is not your mother. But she has a husband like me and a son like you somewhere. If we leave China without rescuing her, she will lose her hope. We don't have a lot of money. But we have enough. Let's save her."

My father and I hired a broker, a human smuggler, and moved the woman to Thailand and then to Seoul. To this day, we are all close friends.

Since then, my father, other defectors, and I have, on our meager salaries, helped rescue other defectors trapped in China. China views North Korean defectors not as refugees fleeing severe human rights abuses but as illegal work migrants. North Koreans caught in China are still deported to Joseon, where they are imprisoned. North Koreans in China live perilous lives, flirting in an underground work economy and suffering abuse, poverty, and depraved living conditions. All they want is freedom.

In the spring of 2015, I became the consultant for the rescuing team of Citizens' Alliance for North Korean Human Rights, a nonprofit group that helps rescue defectors trapped in China. I speak around the world, raising awareness and money to rescue North Koreans in China.

A portion of the proceeds of this book are being donated to the Citizens' Alliance for North Korean Human Rights to help North Korean refugees in China.

IF MYEONGCHUL WERE STILL ALIVE, HE MIGHT SAY, *Don't judge a man until you've walked in his boots.*

Every Shooting Star is my boots. And the boots worn by thousands of other street boys in North Korea and around the world.

This book is for my brothers, Young-bum, Chulho, Min-gook, Unsik, Myeongchul, and Sangchul.

For my grandparents, who never stopped looking for me. They have since died, or so my father and I believe, from natural causes due to old age.

Finally, this book is for my mother. She is still missing. My father and I search for her every day. I will never give up hope that we will be reunited.

ACKNOWLEDGMENTS

I n the summer of 2014, I was living part-time in Ottawa and part-time in Toronto, interning with Barry Devolin, a member of Parliament and deputy speaker of the House of Commons. I was in Canada as the second recipient of the HanVoice Pioneer project, which provides speech, media, and government training to young North Korean defectors.

During this time, I came to meet book and magazine writer Susan Elizabeth McClelland, who had been working as a journalist within the North Korean community in Canada.

Susan and I discussed developing my story into a young adult novel. Susan, author of *Bite of the Mango*, the true story of a young female victim of the Sierra Leone war, felt that young readers—as well as adults—would empathize with my life as a street boy, and would come to see that there are few differences between themselves and children in North Korea, except circumstance. After all, I had, and still have, similar dreams as any child in the world, dreams of love of family and friends and making a difference.

My second spoken language is English. I wrote an outline of my story, starting as a child and ending when I arrived in South Korea. As English is not my first language, I needed Susan to help me flesh out the outline into book chapters. Over the course of many months, Susan and I, through interviews and sending the chapters back and forth, turned the outline into the book you have just read.

Every Falling Star is my childhood story based on my memories of events as they occurred at that time. Please note these were my *childhood* memories when I was a street boy, suffering from trauma, malnutrition, and starvation as well as sleep deprivation. Note also that conversations, while based on my memories, have been re-created for literary effect, as I don't recall them word for word. Also, in some places songs and stories have been altered from their original form and/or telling as, again, I am basing these on what I recollect being told at the time.

This is my story as I remember it. I am told I speak nearly perfect English. However, I know that my spelling and grammar are not as good, and I have no experience in the literary world—writing scenes and dialogue, for instance. With Susan's assistance, I was able to produce the final version, which is what you have in front of you today.

GLOSSARY

Words

abeoji [ah-buh-ᴊɪ] — father

adeul [ah-ᴅᴇᴜʟ] — son

annyeonghaseyo [ahn-ɴʏᴜɴɢ-ha-sae-yo] — hello

binjibpali [bin-ɢᴇᴇ-pali]— people who sell abandoned houses, pretending to own them

boon-dan-we-won-jang [boon-dahn-ᴡᴇ-one-jahng] — class leader

buk [book] — drum

chang [chang] — spear

daejang [dae-ᴊᴀʜɴɢ] — leader of a group or gang

degeori [dae-ge-ʀɪ] — traveling vendors

deodeok [da-ᴅᴏᴄ] — type of root, similar to ginseng, found mostly on the Korean Peninsula and in northern China *dububab* [du-boo-BOB] — rice wrapped with sliced tofu

eomeoni [oh-mo-NI] — mother

gae-gu-ri [GAE-gu-ri] — frog

gamtae [gahm-TAE] — wild berry

gayageum [ga-ya-GUME] — traditional Korean string instrument

guhoso [gu-ho-SO] — detention center for *kotjebi*

hal-abeoji [hal-ah-BUH-ji] — grandfather

hal-meoni [hal-mo-NI] — grandmother

huecos (Spanish) [WAY-cose] — tiny holes into which rock climbers can slip their fingers to help them ascend a steep rock face

jultagi [jool-ta-GI] — street boy who steals clothes from clotheslines

kotjebi [kot-je-BI] — street boy or a homeless boy

omija [oh-mi-JAH] — type of fruit often used in Chinese medicine

pajang-jebi [pa-JAHNG-je-bi] — street boy who steals by knocking over vendors' wares

ping-du [PING-du] — type of illicit drug

ring-nal [RING-nal]— doubled-edged razor blade

sasakki [sa-sah-KI] — Korean card game

seon-saeng-nim [suhn-SENG-nim] — teacher

shan-shin-ryong-nim [shan-SHIN-ryung-nim] — good spirits, thought to live in rocks and certain mountains

shibwon [SHIB-won] — amount of Korean currency

So-nian-jang-soo [so-nyun-JANG-soo] — popular television cartoon in North Korea

so-nyon-dan [so-nyun-DAHN] — organization for children like the Boy Scouts or the Girl Scouts, but heavily involved in North Korean propaganda

sojo [so-JOH] — club

sool [sool] — alcohol

srikoon [sri-KOON] — a *kotjebi* who steals money by cutting open the unsuspecting victim's bag

yaeya [YEH-ya] — little one

yu-ryeong [yoo-RYUNG] — ghosts or evil spirits

Places and proper names

Baekdu-sahn [baek-du-SAHN] — Mountain where Kim Jong-il was alleged to have been born. There is a lake on the top, which is thought to have been created by a meteor. According to folklore, the mountain is a sign that the Korean people have been touched by heaven.

Kang Ban-sok [kang bahn-SOK] — Kim Il-sung's mother

Cheongjin [chung-JIN] — provincial capital of North Hamgyeong, with four markets: Pohwang, Sunam, Ranam, Songpyeong

Chilseong [chil-SUNG] — Name of a deity. There are different versions of the origins of Chilseong, depending on where in Asia someone lives. Sungju's father told him that Chilseong was a heavenly figure who descended to earth and, when she and her daughters died, returned to heaven and became the Big Dipper.

Daedong-gang [deh-dong-GANG] — river that runs through Pyongyang

"Dondolari" [don-dol-LA-ri] —Korean folk song

Duman-gang [doo-mahn-gang] — river that divides China and North Korea

Eodaejin [uh-dae-JIN] — port city

Heungbu wa Nolbu [hung-BU WAH nol-BU] — Characters in a Korean folk story about two brothers. Heungbu was poor. He chased away a snake that had injured a swallow and helped the swallow heal. In exchange, the swallow gave Heungbu a gourd, the seeds of which granted him great wealth. The other brother, Nolbu, was rich. He became jealous of Heungbu, so he injured a swallow and then helped it heal, hoping to gain the same richness. Instead, the seeds of his gourd brought him nothing but pain and misery.

Joseon [jo-SUHN] — North Korea

Joseon Inmingun [jo-SUHN in-min-GOON] — Korean army; also the name of a newspaper of the Korean Army

Mangyeongdae [mahn-gyung-dae] — village where Kim Il-sung was born

Mangyeongdae Yuheejang [mahn-gyung-dae you-hee-JAHNG] — famous North Korean amusement park

Rodong Sinmun [ro-dong shin-MOON] — newspaper of the Central Committee of the Worker's Party of Korea

"Shagwa-poongnyon" [sha-gwa poong-NYUN] — Korean song

Sup'ung Dam [su-poong dam] — dam on the Yalu river, built by the Japanese starting in 1937